# *Finally*
# Organized
# *Finally*
# Free

## *Maria Gracia*

# Finally Organized, Finally Free

# Finally Organized, Finally Free

### by Maria Gracia

Get Organized Now!

http://www.getorganizednow.com

BlueMoon Publishing
Milwaukee, WI

Published by **BlueMoon Publishing.**

Copyright ©1999 by Maria Gracia.

Editor: Joseph G. Gracia

Cover Design: Joseph G. Gracia

Interior Clipart: Microsoft Publisher™, Microsoft Graphics Studio Greetings 99™ and Lotus Smartpics™

Please direct any comments, questions or suggestions regarding this book to:

BlueMoon Publishing
5650 West Wahner Avenue #214
PO Box 240398
Milwaukee, WI 53223-9015, U.S.A.

(414) 354-5891
ebscompany@aol.com

**Library of Congress Cataloging-in-Publication Data**

Gracia, Maria
    Finally Organized, Finally Free/by Maria Gracia
    ISBN # 0-9672795-0-X  $29.95

    Library of Congress Catalog Card Number 99-90594

    Includes Index.

    Reference: Home Organization, Personal Organization, Office Organization, Goals, Self-Help, Business Resources, Time Management, Planning, Achievement

ISBN # 0-9672795-0-X

Printed in the United States of America

## *Dedication*

This book is dedicated to my loving husband,
business partner and best friend,
Joe Gracia,
a constant source of love, motivation
and inspiration.

## *With special thanks*

To my mother, father and sister,
Margie, Mike and Jude,
who have always inspired me with their hard work,
dedication, love and support.

# CONTENTS

# Introduction

*I've got to get organized!*

When did you last utter these words? Maybe it was when you realized that the raging, paper beast had taken complete control over your office or home.

Possibly the words came—along with a slew of some "not-so-nice" words—as you desperately searched for those missing theater or ball game tickets.

Perhaps you said it when you finally gave in to the fact that you just have *too much stuff*. You may have even contemplated tossing everything out the window!

It could have been when you missed that important appointment. Or when that deadline crept up on you.

Or even worst, it may have happened when you found out you had no time left for yourself, your family, your friends, that needed vacation and basically everything in life that you love to do.

You're not alone. Those words have been expressed over and over again by thousands.

Disorganization can actually *trap* you into living a life filled with stress, frustration and chaos. It can rob you of the precious time you should be spending enjoying your life.

By overcoming disorganization, you can be set *free* to live the kind of life you've always dreamed of.

> **The triumph over anything is a matter of organization.**
>
> Jacques Attali

My husband, Joe, and I run our own home-based business. Believe me, we have a lot of work, reams of paper and thousands of computer files. Our phone is constantly ringing off the hook. We generate an average of 100 e-mails a day—most of which require quick responses. We have appointments and meetings that take us on the road. Our mailbox is, to make a slight understatement, bursting!

However, besides running our business—which, by the way, we love to do—we have plenty of time to keep in contact with our family and friends. We go out to romantic dinners. Vacations and mini-vacations are taken often. Long nature walks, in addition to healthy power walks, are a regular activity. There's plenty of time to watch our favorite television programs and to read interesting novels. Our meals are home-cooked and healthy. There's even time to get 7-8 hours of restful sleep each night.

And the funny thing is, we have just as much time as you do. All of us are blessed with 24 hours a day and all of us have a choice as to how we spend that time.

No thanks to the lousy million dollar lottery odds, the majority of us must work to survive. Nevertheless, we can all make time in our lives for the things that really count.

*You* have to be the one to select those things that are important to you. Getting organized is really a personal quest to save as much time as you can for the things that matter most. And the only way to *save time*, is to *waste less of it*.

> *A journey of a thousand miles must begin with a single step.*
>
> Lao-tzu

## Things in our lives that waste our time

*"If I only had more time."*

*"I didn't get much done today."*

*"The only way I'll catch up is if I don't go to sleep—for a year!"*

*"I've got enough scheduled for three lifetimes!"*

*"Where did all the time go?"*

*"It couldn't be late already. I just got started."*

*"I need more time."*

These phrases have been spoken by millions. So, where is all our time going? Here is a small list of some things in our lives that absorb our precious time. How many are directly related to your life?

| | | | |
|---|---|---|---|
| ___ | Messy, cluttered office | ___ | Messy, cluttered desktop |
| ___ | Messy, cluttered home | ___ | Paper piles |
| ___ | No priorities | ___ | Conflicting priorities |
| ___ | Procrastination | ___ | Unnecessary delays |
| ___ | Lack of discipline | ___ | Lack of feedback |
| ___ | Resistance to change | ___ | Hasty decisions |
| ___ | Preoccupation | ___ | Lack of sleep |
| ___ | Lack of nutrition | ___ | Lack of exercise |
| ___ | Lack of order | ___ | Unexpected phone calls |
| ___ | Unexpected visitors | ___ | Long phone calls |
| ___ | Telephone Tag | ___ | No goals |
| ___ | Poorly defined goals | ___ | Fear of offending |

| | |
|---|---|
| __ Mistakes | __ Unrealistic time estimates |
| __ Excessive socializing | __ Insufficient delegation |
| __ Ineffective delegation | __ Arguing, dueling |
| __ Distracting objects | __ Too involved in details |
| __ Tendency to do too much | __ Overlap of responsibilities |
| __ Unclear roles | __ Inability to terminate visits |
| __ Unscheduled maintenance | __ Interruptions |
| __ Distractions | __ Not listening |
| __ Lack of communication | __ Miscommunication |
| __ Confused priorities | __ Slow reading |
| __ Incomprehensive reading | __ Lack of authority |
| __ No planning | __ Insufficient planning |
| __ Rationalization | __ Failure to set deadlines |
| __ Negative attitude | __ Failure to anticipate |
| __ Associates stopping by to chat | __ Open door policies |
| __ More than one boss | __ Poorly trained employees |
| __ Lack of competent staff | __ Most business lunches |
| __ Meetings with undefined goals | __ Overstaffing |
| __ Understaffing | __ Lack of company policy |
| __ Lack of home rules | __ Restricting everything to memory alone |

> *Don't put it down.*
> *Put it away.*
>
> Kathy Peel

You're about to discover over 1,300 tips that will help eliminate those things that are wasting your time, cluttering your life and hindering you from doing the things you love to do. That's what this book, *Finally Organized, Finally Free,* is all about.

## Start off on the right foot

Right now, I'm going to ask you to determine exactly what it is you're trying to accomplish by reading this book. The more specific you are in your description, the easier it will be for you to succeed in achieving your objectives.

For example, stating, "I'd like to eliminate clutter," is too broad.

It would be better to say, "I'd like to remove every piece of paper from my desktop and create an effective filing system, so that I can find anything I need in 30 seconds or less."

Or how about, "I'd like to set up a family schedule so that everyone has an equal amount of chores and everyone knows where another family member is at any given time."

You get the point. Take a moment right now to think about and write down your personal objectives.

My objectives are:

*To be organized means:*

*1) You get everything done when it's due.*

*2) You find everything you need when you need it.*

Maria Gracia

1. _____

_____

_____

2. _____

_____

_____

3. _____

_____

_____

4. _____

_____

_____

The next critical step is to set a practical deadline to accomplish each of these objectives. So, go back to each one and assign a *specific* date that you wish to meet each of them. Saying, "as soon as possible" is too broad. It must be a calendar date such as September 26 or July 7.

Setting objectives and deadlines gives you something to shoot for. If you don't meet your goals by your deadlines, that doesn't mean that you have failed. It just means you have to re-adjust your deadlines and go for it once again, until you've achieved your objectives.

## How to use this book

*Finally Organized, Finally Free* begins by introducing the 10 Personality Styles. Once you discover what style(s) best describe you, you'll be able to apply the organizational systems that work in harmony with your personality.

From there on, this book is categorized into individual topics, each segment covering a different aspect of your life. There are tips, ideas and real life question/answer sessions within each to help you save time. Some can help you save a few minutes; some, a few hours. Nevertheless, they are all designed to help you get better organized.

Choose a few tips and ideas at a time. Don't try to implement dozens at once. Realize that effective organization is an ongoing process. Once you begin to execute one of these ideas, continue to practice it over and over again. Soon enough, each tip or idea that you institute will become a habit. By the way, only after you do something repetitively, a total of 21 times, does it become a habit and part of your everyday routine.

Each idea, tip, technique and system you use will bring you another step closer to achieving organizational success. Just as you learned everything else in life—one step at a time—so too will you be able to say that you're *Finally Organized, Finally Free.*

This is not something to be achieved in a day. Getting organized requires knowledge, implementation, practice and motivation just as it does to effectively ride a bike, play golf or cook a meal. However, taking it one step at a time, while maintaining an "I can do it" attitude, will get you there before you know it.

You can do it. I wish you the greatest success in getting organized, so that you can be *Finally Organized, Finally Free*!

*Put your hand on a hot stove for a minute and it seems like an hour.*

*Sit with a pretty girl for an hour and it seems like a minute.*

*That's relativity.*

Albert Einstein

# Chapter 1

❖ ❖ ❖ ❖ ❖ ❖ ❖ ❖ ❖ ❖ ❖ ❖ ❖ ❖ ❖ ❖

# Personality Styles

E very person has his or her own personality. Our personalities make us unique as a society. After all, the world would be a boring place if we were all exactly the same.

However, when it comes to organization, there are common traits that we all share. I've taken these similar aspects and categorized them into *Personality Styles*.

Five of these Personality Styles are "time" related, while the other five are "space" related.

On the following few pages, you will find Personality Style Surveys and Scoring Instructions.

You may want to make copies of these surveys so that other people in your life can also fill them out.

Simply take the survey and determine your score. You'll soon discover what your individual Personality Style(s) are.

Every style is described in more detail on the pages following the surveys. The organizing tips and ideas contained in each are specifically designed to work in harmony with your particular style(s).

After you and others take the surveys, you'll probably discover that each person falls into their own unique style(s). This helps everyone to understand each other a little better and also to recognize why one way of organizing may work for one person and why another person may need to take a different approach.

The great news is, each of these Personality Styles can be organized!

Once you learn and apply the organizing systems that coordinate with each style, you can then select other systems that work *with*, rather than *against*, your individual Personality Style(s).

---

*Efficiency is doing things right.*

*Effectiveness is doing the right things.*

Peter Drucker

# Time Organization Survey

*On the line that follows each question below, indicate the number that most accurately describes you best, according to the following choices. Then, add up your scores for each individual section and write your total on the TOTAL line. After the survey has been completed and scored, transfer your scores to the Survey Results Form.*

*10 = Always*　　　　*8 = Often*　　　　*5 = Sometimes*　　　　*2 = Seldom*　　　　*0 = Never*

## Time 1 ............................................................................................................ Total ___

1.  Do you get bored if you don't have a variety of things going on at one time? _____
2.  Do you feel you get little accomplished in a day, even though you're working on several tasks? _____
3.  Do you drop projects or tasks you're working on to do something else? _____
4.  Do you leave projects or tasks incomplete? _____
5.  Do you do things on a whim, instead of in a scheduled manner? _____
6.  Do you easily forget where you placed items? _____
7.  Do you feel you're easily distracted? _____
8.  Do you feel you don't have enough time in the day to get everything done? _____
9.  Do you feel that if you're not busy, you're not being productive? _____
10. Do you begin working on something in one room and wind up in another without knowing when and how you got there? _____

## Time 2 ............................................................................................................ Total ___

11. Do you get "very annoyed" when in the same room with a person who is disorganized? _____
12. Do you rewrite letters or memos over and over until you get them just right? _____
13. Do you miss deadlines because you get heavily involved in details? _____
14. When presenting something, do you feel it's essential to mention every detail to support a point? _____
15. Do you feel very frustrated when you don't get to every item on your To Do List? _____
16. Do you rarely skim when you read, due to constant fear that you may miss a critical detail? _____
17. After completing a project or task, do you often feel you could have done it better? _____
18. Do you work endless hours even if the projects are not due anytime soon? _____
19. Do you feel very frustrated when people don't stick to an established schedule? _____
20. Do you avoid delegating projects, because you feel they won't get done the way you want them to? _____

## Time 3 ............................................................................................................ Total ___

21. Do you prefer coming up with the general idea, rather than working out the details? _____
22. When you assign a project to someone, do you generally describe the desired outcome of the project and then leave the execution to someone else? _____
23. Do you feel that tidying up is generally a waste of time? _____
24. Do you feel frustrated when you have to take time reviewing detailed analyses? _____
25. Do you to leave important items behind when you leave work or your house because you're in a constant rush? _____
26. Do you prefer to deliver a message in person or by phone, rather that writing it by hand? _____
27. Do you tend to forget meetings and appointments? _____
28. Do you prefer to delegate routine correspondence, rather than doing it yourself? _____
29. Do you get impatient with people who need to tell you the details about something? _____
30. Do you feel uncomfortable with anything that involves lots of detail? _____

## Time 4 ............................................................................................................ Total ___

31. Do you have trouble making decisions on most things? _____
32. Do you put off making decisions, even after you've researched every last detail? _____
33. Do you sometimes fear choosing one option over another, because you feel whatever you choose might be wrong? _____
34. Do you have difficulty ranking your priorities? _____
35. Do you feel you "never" have enough information to make a good decision? _____
36. Do you give yourself too many alternatives from which to choose? _____
37. Do you always hold back on decisions because of the risks involved? _____
38. Do you constantly worry about whether you made the right decision? _____
39. Do you take so long to make a decision that you miss some favorable opportunities? _____
40. Do you let others make important decisions that affect you? _____

## Time 5 ............................................................................................................ Total ___

41. Do you like waiting until the last minute to begin things? _____
42. Do you generally need to be pressured to complete a task? _____
43. Do you generally find yourself rushing to attend events, get to a meeting, etc? _____
44. Do you feel that stress helps you to be more alert and to think more clearly and perceptively? _____
45. Do you tend to get bored when things are going too smoothly? _____
46. Do you run around in a last-minute rush more than 2 times a week? _____
47. Do you wait until the last minute to buy gifts? _____
48. Do you involve others in a race to help you meet deadlines? _____
49. Do you feel exhilarated after completing an important project just before the deadline? _____
50. Do you have more motivation and drive when you have outside pressure? _____

# Space Organization Survey

*On the line that follows each question below, indicate the number that most accurately describes you best, according to the following choices. Then, add up your scores for each individual section and write your total on the TOTAL line. After the survey has been completed and scored, transfer your scores to the Survey Results Form.*

**10 = Always        8 = Often        5 = Sometimes        2 = Seldom        0 = Never**

## Space 1 ......................................................................................... Total ____

1. Do you prefer keeping things out in the open so you won't forget them? .............. _____
2. Do you like to display Post-it notes all over your office? ......................... _____
3. Do you feel it's a waste of time putting things away if you're going to use them within the next few days? ..... _____
4. Do you fear that if you put things away, you may not find them later when you need them? ..... _____
5. Do you like to surround yourself with "lots" of pictures, inspirational thoughts or cartoons, etc? ..... _____
6. When working on a long-term project, do you prefer spreading everything out you might need, leaving it there until you're finished? ..... _____
7. Do you feel uncomfortable if your surroundings are totally empty? ..... _____
8. Do you see piles of paper as evidence that you're working hard? ..... _____
9. When you don't know what to do with a piece of paper, do you prefer leaving it on top of your desk? ..... _____
10. Do you like things to stare you in the face so you'll constantly be reminded of how much work you have to do? ..... _____

## Space 2 ......................................................................................... Total ____

11. Do you hate to see clutter? ..... _____
12. Does having a clear space make you feel as though you're more in control? ..... _____
13. Do you equate a clear surface with a clear mind? ..... _____
14. Do you shove everything out of sight before associates or guests arrive? ..... _____
15. Do you prefer to have nothing on your desk, except what you need to work with at the moment? ..... _____
16. Do you like using boxes and other organizational tools that help keep things from view? ..... _____
17. Do you like writing things down in a notebook, instead of on individual pieces of paper? ..... _____
18. Do you like to put things away immediately after using them? ..... _____
19. Does putting things back where they belong make you feel as though you're accomplishing something? ..... _____
20. Do you feel better putting things away, rather than leaving everything out at all times? ..... _____

## Space 3 ......................................................................................... Total ____

21. Do you save things even if you have no use for them? ..... _____
22. Do you hesitate to throw something out because someone else might have a use for it? ..... _____
23. Do you hang onto things because you don't know what else to do with them? ..... _____
24. Do you feel sentimental about most of the items you possess? ..... _____
25. Do you feel your home or office is running out of storage space? ..... _____
26. Do people ever wonder why you save as many things as you do? ..... _____
27. Do you keep clothes that you never wear and probably never will again? ..... _____
28. Do you feel more secure keeping "everything," rather than discarding "anything?" ..... _____
29. Do you put aside things that are broken with the expectation that you'll get them fixed someday? ..... _____
30. Do you frequent garage sales and flea markets? ..... _____

## Space 4 ......................................................................................... Total ____

31. Do you feel you have to constantly straighten things up? ..... _____
32. Do you feel it's important to have nice looking surroundings, even if the area is not very efficient? ..... _____
33. When you're under pressure, does it make you feel better to tidy things up? ..... _____
34. Do you identify with Felix Unger, the perfectionist, from the television series *The Odd Couple*? ..... _____
35. Do you find yourself constantly arranging things a certain way on tables and shelves? ..... _____
36. Do you feel annoyed when people move things out of their proper place? ..... _____
37. When people temporarily move an item out of its place, do you feel compelled to move it back? ..... _____
38. Does it annoy you when pictures are crooked? ..... _____
39. If you had to rearrange your surroundings, due to unforeseen circumstances, would you feel annoyed? ..... _____
40. If something is a real mess, do you tend to stay away from it until you can clean it up totally? ..... _____

## Space 5 ......................................................................................... Total ____

41. Do you have to step over piles of paper to get to your desk? ..... _____
42. Do other people complain about your sloppiness? ..... _____
43. Do you identify with Oscar Madison, from the television series *The Odd Couple*, who stuffed his brown tie into one of his brown shoes to keep track of it? ..... _____
44. Does it bother you when you're asked to pick up after yourself? ..... _____
45. Do you agree that "A neat desk is a sure sign of a sick mind"? ..... _____
46. Does it seem like too much effort to put things back after you use them? ..... _____
47. Do you avoid cleaning at all costs? ..... _____
48. Do you have trouble understanding why other people are bothered by a mess? ..... _____
49. Do you look at a cluttered room and not see the clutter? ..... _____
50. Do you feel that it's a total waste of time keeping things neat? ..... _____

## Time and Space Organization
## Survey Results Form

*Indicate your scores from the Time and Space Organization Surveys below.*

### *Time Organization Survey Styles*

Time 1 .........................Drop and Hop........................ _____

Time 2 .........................Perfectionist........................ _____

Time 3 .........................Detail Dodger........................ _____

Time 4 .........................Fence Sitter........................ _____

Time 5 .........................Cliff Hanger........................ _____

### *Space Organization Survey Styles*

Space 1 .........................Out and About........................ _____

Space 2 .........................Minimalist........................ _____

Space 3 .........................Pack Rat........................ _____

Space 4 .........................Neat Nik........................ _____

Space 5 .........................Oscar Madison........................ _____

*Next, use the following key to determine what your tendency percent is in each style.*

*Greater than 69% = High tendencies*     *21-69% = Some tendencies*     *Less than 21% = Low tendencies*

**Chapter 2**

# Time Personality Styles

# Drop and Hop

Start a project, get bored, hop on to something else. That's the motto of the Drop and Hop. The thrill and excitement of doing something new is what gets the Drop and Hop through the day. Sound good? Sometimes. But the adverse effect is often that the Drop and Hop gets little accomplished in his or her day. Many tasks are started, but most never get completed.

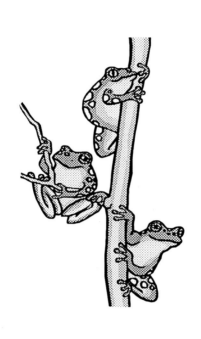

- To keep on top of everything you have to do, always use both Master Lists and To Do Lists.

- Watches with alarms, kitchen timers and other triggering devices will alert you when you're not sticking to your priorities. Set them at half-hour intervals to remind you to check if you're on track.

- Since you can be easily distracted, try using visual reminders whenever possible. Perhaps, creating and posting a sign with the following questions will help you decide . . .

    ✓ Does the interruption really need to be handled immediately?

    ✓ Can this interruption be deterred until a later date?

    ✓ Can this interruption be diverted to someone else?

- When interrupted, jot down a short note to remind yourself where you left off. You'll get back on track quickly, without wasting time.

- Minimize distractions. Close the door. Put up a **Do Not Disturb** sign. Establish specific periods when you're available to speak with people. Create written instructions and checklists so everyone knows what to do without interrupting you.

- Break projects down into bite-sized pieces that can be completed in a shorter span of time. This way, you can schedule your time to work on a variety of projects and still accomplish what you need to.

- Place time limits on phone calls and visitors so they don't take over the time that could have been spent working on your priorities. Say, "I've only got 5 minutes to talk to you."

# Perfectionist

Perfectionists give 100% attention to *everything* they do. This kind of dedication is quite honorable. The one thing that many Perfectionists fail to do though, is determine what *really* deserves that much attention. For instance, achieving financial freedom should probably warrant more attention than solving a crossword puzzle.

Perfectionists put so much time into trivial and minor details that they tend to work endless hours and still miss deadlines.

- There's a very fine line between *high-standards* and *superhuman expectations*. Determine if you could *really* complete a task to your satisfaction by the date that you've set for yourself.

  Heavily pad the time frame you schedule to complete a project because you'll frequently estimate less time than your high standards need. Instead of scheduling fifteen minutes, schedule a half hour. Rather than scheduling two days, allow at least three days.

- Just say "No." You don't have unlimited time. You don't have unlimited resources. You have to respect your time. If you don't, nobody else will.

- Perfectionists with too many high-priority items on their agendas will fall behind. Limit your high-priority projects to a maximum of two at a time. Don't take on more than you can handle.

- Delegate. You can't do *everything* yourself and give everything 100%. Train your staff—if you're fortunate enough to have one— and delegate to them. If you don't have a staff, there are plenty of companies and individuals that you may be able to outsource to.

- Prioritize. If you try to give 100% attention to everything, you're going to have a hard time getting anything done. Determine what your most important projects are and give those the time they deserve. Other less important projects can be delayed until the vital tasks are accomplished, delegated to someone else or outsourced.

- Perfectionists have a tendency to spend time fretting over every tiny detail. While this is absolutely necessary with some projects, it is certainly not needed in all cases. Determine what's really worth your in-depth attention.

- Keep in mind, in the real world there isn't time to aspire to perfection in *all* things that you do. When you attempt to do everything at the highest possible standard, there are hundreds of things that you'll never get to do. Prioritize. Spend more quality time on the things that contribute to your goals and dreams and less time on those items that do not.

# Detail Dodger

Details, details. "I'm not a detail person." This is fine when competent people are already handling those pesky details. Thank goodness for the detail people, otherwise we wouldn't have a Disneyworld, a stock market or indoor plumbing!

The Detail Dodger has a tendency to forget. Appointments are missed. Meetings are forgotten. Deadlines are ignored. Other people are often forced to pick up the pieces that have fallen through the cracks.

- Write it down. When your thought is on paper, it doesn't have to be stored in your memory. You're sure to remember every detail.

- Get help remembering all those details. An assistant can help keep you on top of everything. You can also use computer software, such as Microsoft Outlook™, that sounds off an alarm when meetings, appointments and other important events are coming up.

- Use the "Never Forget Reminder System" to recall each detail easily. This no-fail system is explained later in this book.

- Make written or typed lists of all the standard and recurring things you need to remember, categorized by subject. For example, create lists for grocery shopping, packing, errands, projects due and more.

- Tack up visual reminders where you can't possibly miss them; areas that are constantly in view. A note on your office door, telephone, mirror or car steering wheel can catch your eye quickly and help you remember those details.

- Do similar tasks at the same time each day. Having a consistent schedule will make it easier for you to remember what needs to be done. For example, if you have to make sales calls, you may plan to make all of them each day between 4:00 and 5:00. If you have to file, plan on filing every Friday at 3:00.

- A very long To Do List frequently looks intimidating to the Detail Dodger, therefore many items never get completed. Schedule no more than 4 Vital Tasks in any given day. Don't start anything else until they're done.

# Fence Sitter

Fence Sitters hope and pray that they won't have to choose. They fear making the wrong decision, so they settle on avoiding it, at all costs. Fence Sitters wait so long, that favorable opportunities are often missed. They procrastinate, while the world is passing them by. Fence Sitters depend on other people to make decisions for them. They often fail to control their own destinies.

- Fence Sitters are overwhelmed and intimidated by large projects. Therefore they never make the decision to start them. Break it down into bite-sized pieces. Get a bunch of index cards. First, determine the end result and write that goal on one card. Then, jot down each other step that must be accomplished using one card per step. These don't have to be in any particular order yet. When all the steps are written down, arrange the index cards in the appropriate sequence. Finally, tackle the job, card by card.

- Use a Pro/Con list. Do this for each possible scenario. Then, choose the one that ends up with the most pros and the least cons.

- Get input from a friend, family member, associate or expert. Ask them how they would handle it. Get feedback and add these viewpoints to your Pro/Con list.

- Don't overload yourself with too much information. The more choices you have, the more difficult the decision will be. Imagine going to a restaurant and looking at a menu with six options versus one hundred! Get the information you need to make an educated decision, but don't go overboard. Narrow down your choices.

- If you don't have a specific deadline, decision making could be dragged out for months. Assign a deadline, write it on your calendar and force yourself to make a decision once the date arrives.

- You will run into situations when you're really not sure whether or not a decision you make will result in a favorable outcome. Generally, there is not "one" right decision. It's better to make any decision, than no decision at all. Learn to say, "that's life." Flip a coin, make a decision and let whatever happens be. You'll always be in control of your own destiny.

# Cliff Hanger

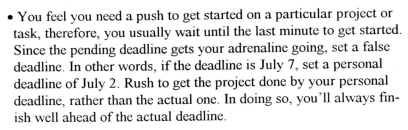

Y ou're watching a movie and all of a sudden you've reached it. That final burst of energy that happens, just before the plot is finalized. Sheer excitement? Only in the movies. Cliff Hanger personality types wait until the very last minute to start something. They wait for pressure to get moving. Cliff Hangers think they're getting everyone exhilarated with this last minute burst. But in reality, they're driving everyone crazy!

- You feel you need a push to get started on a particular project or task, therefore, you usually wait until the last minute to get started. Since the pending deadline gets your adrenaline going, set a false deadline. In other words, if the deadline is July 7, set a personal deadline of July 2. Rush to get the project done by your personal deadline, rather than the actual one. In doing so, you'll always finish well ahead of the actual deadline.

- Cliff Hangers often underestimate the time it will take to complete a project. This results in starting the project too late and then missing deadlines. When you are scheduling, pad each project or task. Add another hour or another day. If you finish the project ahead of time, great! If not, you'll still have more time before your deadline.

- Don't keep everything you have to do, stored in your memory. Make a Master List of everything you have to do. Then, simply transfer the most important ones to your To Do List and work on those first. Evaluate both your Master List and your To Do List once a day to ensure the important projects are getting the attention they need.

- Break your goals down into mini-goals with rewards for each. As you accomplish each goal, reward yourself. You'll get all the inspiration and excitement you need to keep going.

- Cliff Hangers often need pressure to start a task. For that extra boost of excitement, play "Beat the Clock." To get moving, set a timer for 10 minutes and work like mad. See how much you can get done in that short burst of time and reward yourself if you've accomplished what you thought you could do.

- If you have an extensive amount of work, delegate whatever possible to people who can handle it. Designate a specific time each day—at least 15 minutes—to review your projects and to determine what you could give to someone else to complete. Don't let the project just sit on your desk for days and then stress somebody else with a job that should have been started much earlier.

# Chapter 3

# Space Personality Styles

# Out and About

Out and About Personalities believe that *out of sight is out of mind*. They avoid putting anything away, even when not being used, for fear that they'll never find it again. Out and Abouts believe that if everything is out in view, they'll never lose anything. At least, that's the theory. In reality, as more and more items are left out in the open, they work their way under other things and vanish.

- Use open desk trays and baskets to keep everything out in the open and organized at the same time. Buy different colors for each category or person. Clearly label each so you always know what goes inside and what doesn't.

- Use open pen/pencil caddies. If you don't have a specific place for your daily supplies—pens, pencils, highlighters, markers, scissors—they will get lost. Buy one with a number of compartments that allows you to separate each item into groups.

- Use open vertical file sorters. Putting everything into filing cabinets may not be a satisfying choice for the Out and About. It is recommended that you put most files away in filing cabinets, but keep your daily and weekly files out in the open in vertical file sorters. Effective filing rules apply here: categorize, alphabetize, color-code and label.

- Use open Rolodex™ card files. Instead of using Post-it™ notes all over the place, keep your friends and associates in a Rolodex™ card file. Place it right near your phone for easy access.

- For small items that you need to keep in clear view, a plastic, translucent case—such as a child's zippered pencil case—is an excellent way to effectively serve your needs.

- Create a Visible Phone Message Center with a bulletin board, phone message slips and push pins. Details later in this book.

- Hang it up. Use lucite wall pockets. Install wall shelves. Attach large, erasable planning calendars to the wall. Hang framed pictures and other inspirational items.

# Minimalist

Doesn't this desk look like an ice skating rink?! Unlike Out and Abouts, Minimalists detest anything out in the open and equate a clear space with a clear mind. This is great, except when they stuff everything they own into a closet or drawer with no rhyme or reason. Then, when the time arrives to find something, they're out of luck.

- Since you like paper out of view, it is vital to create an effective filing system. Details are explained later in this book.

- Use planners with fold-in sections and inserts. While everything is inside, all items are still accessible within seconds.

- Use a Palm Pilot™ or an all-in-one computer software planner, such as Microsoft Outlook™, to keep schedules, lists, addresses and more all in one compact unit.

- Rolltop desks hide all from view when not being used. Desks with a flip-up panel are also a preferred choice of this Personality Style.

- Since you are probably going to keep most of your supplies in your desk, be sure to use separators and dividers whenever possible.

- Furniture with built-in storage space is a great choice for the Minimalist. Choose cabinets with doors that close, benches with storage space under the seat and desks with lots of drawers.

- Keep day to day work in your computer, rather than on paper. Create type-in forms and templates. Write e-mail instead of written notes. Use a computer card file for addresses and phone numbers.

- Organizing storage containers come in all shapes, sizes and colors. The translucent ones allow you to see everything inside. Categorize each similar group of items into their own clearly labeled container.

- Make a map or list detailing where you've hidden everything. When you need to find something, simply pull it out. You'll be able to locate whatever you need in minutes.

# Pack Rat

The wonderful, sentimental Pack Rat. So nice. So loveable. So out of space! Pack Rats desperately need more room, but can't bear to part with their stuff. There are boxes of old records, books since grade school, reams of outdated paperwork, matchbooks from 20 years of weddings, decades of clothing, plus that horrible artwork from dear Aunt Martha, taking up every last nook and cranny of space. I've known Pack Rats that are literally possessed by their possessions!

- If you save things you feel you may use someday, create a "May Come in Handy Someday" box. Place those things inside and when the box is full, discard something before you put anything else in.

- Use the "Rotation Box" system. Instead of displaying everything you like at once, display a little bit at a time. Keep the rest boxed up in storage. Every few months, put a few of these things in your box and take a few other things out for display.

- Have you ever put aside broken items with the expectation that you'll get them fixed one day? Chances are, these items are still where you left them and they're still broken. Immediately schedule a date on your calendar and repair them when the date rolls around or toss the items right now while you have it on your mind.

- If it disturbs you to throw something out, even if you're never going to use it again, consider passing it on to someone else. Ask friends, family or associates if they want it. If not, donate it. Your local Salvation Army will probably take it, as long as the condition is fairly good. Remember, your trash is another person's treasure.

- Avoid the "Halfway-house Syndrome." You know, that's when you put things aside that you're not sure what to do with. These temporary storage areas almost always turn into permanent storage. Force yourself to make a decision whether to keep or toss.

- Next time you're wondering if you should keep or toss, take the simple "Keep or Toss" test. It's described in detail later.

- Take photographs of possessions you don't want to forget, but don't have the space for. Save the photos in a scrapbook. Keep the memory, rather than allowing the memory to take up space.

# Neat-Nik

Neat-Niks want everything to look neat. They spend endless hours straightening things. They stack paperwork across their tables and desks, as if they were just about to play a relaxing game of solitaire. However, just because someone is *neat*, does not necessarily mean they're organized.

Even if something is in a neat pile, chances are the Neat-Nik won't have a clue as to what is contained in that pile! Neat-Niks also have an uncanny knack for convincing themselves and others that *form* is more important than *function*.

- Use organizing tools that will keep things both neat *and* organized. Containers with individual compartments will allow you to group similar items together, while separating them from those items they don't belong with.

- Neat-Niks avoid doing a job because they may not be able to finish it in one fell swoop, therefore they just feel better leaving it in a neat pile until they can get to it. Unfortunately, that reasoning is just going to allow that pile to grow larger. Tackle the job a little at a time. Remove a little from the pile and either toss it or store it in a more appropriate area. In the meantime, your pile will still be neat, but will get smaller and smaller with each passing day until it has completely vanished.

- Let's say you have a pile of photographs that are tossed neatly in a photo box. They're certainly neat, but can you find a photograph when you're looking for one without sorting through every single photo? That's the difference between *form* and *function*. You're serving the form part of the equation, so you're halfway there. Now, if you buy index dividers for your photo box and separate your photos by year or event, you'll be accomplishing both form *and* function.

- Don't take up every last space on your desk by lining up paper for each project that you have to do, like a game of solitaire. Use clearly labeled file folders and store them neatly in a vertical file sorter. You'll be satisfying your Neat-Nik tendencies, plus keeping everything easily accessible when needed.

- Felix Unger—the super neat character from *The Odd Couple*—was compulsively neat. If you can identify with Felix and your neat extremes have become an obsession, remember, life is too short to be straightening every minute. Don't allow organizing and cleaning up to become an obsession, otherwise it will take over your life and you'll never have time for the important things.

# Oscar Madison

Oscar Madison! Need I say more? You remember him, don't you? He's the loveable *(messy)* sports writer from the TV hit series *The Odd Couple*—faithful roommate of Felix Unger. The home and office of the Oscar Madison style appears to have been involved in a devastating hurricane or tornado. To put it mildly, it's nearly an impossible feat for Oscar to find anything within the clutter.

- Oscar Madison Personality Styles often have a mess because they feel they have better things to do than to organize and clean. However, they are often embarrassed when someone stops by to visit and sees the mess. To avoid this embarrassment, get a professional organizer or a friend to help you get organized. Then hire someone on a week to week basis to keep you on track.

- Use disposable items whenever possible. For example, instead of using dishes, glasses and silverware that all need to be washed, use paper plates, paper cups and plastic utensils that can be dumped as soon as you're finished using them.

- Eliminate paper from your life as much as possible. Use your computer hard drive, disks and CD-roms to store your files. Send e-mail instead of written notes. Request that others send you e-mail instead of paper. Use a Palm Pilot™ or an all-in-one computer contact manager such as Microsoft Outlook™ to hold your addresses, lists, calendar, appointments and more.

- Hire an assistant who is super-organized. He or she could keep you on track, alert you to appointments and handle your filing. However, don't expect this person to clean up after you. If you need that sort of service, hire a maid or a cleaning service.

- Sometimes, the Oscar Madison can't organize due to lack of organizing knowledge. In addition to this book, there are other sources available. For example, the internet is loaded with organizing tips and storage solutions. A professional organizer can offer practical ideas and systems. Get help and you'll have less clutter, you'll avoid embarrassment and live your life with less stress.

- People form opinions about you based on the cleanliness and organization of your home or office. When visitors stop by, they'll immediately decide how much you care about a number of things just by looking at your surroundings. If you want people to look at you as someone who takes pride in everything they do, organizing and cleaning up will be an enormous help in leaving this impression.

## Chapter 4

# Family Matters

With all the activities the typical family is involved in these days, it's a wonder that we can get anything done. Besides work, school and household chores, there are softball games, choir practice sessions, gymnastics, soccer meets, PTA meetings, town boards, ballet lessons, book clubs, business socials and an endless roster of other things filling up our schedules.

We have to organize family time so that everyone can do the *individual* things they love to do, but we also need time to spend *with each other*. This involves creatively scheduling and planning ahead, eliminating those things that waste time uselessly and involving the entire family in the things that need to get done.

• Schedule frequent dates with your spouse, children and significant others. Write these appointments on your calendar and do everything you can so that they don't have to be rescheduled or put on the backburner. Effective organization ensures you don't ever forget to make time for those you love.

• Do multiple activities simultaneously. Go for a walk in the park with your spouse and/or children. You'll be communicating, exercising and possibly planning for that long needed vacation—all at the same time!

• Create a "Family Message Center." Use a corkboard, message paper and push pins. Place it in a prominent place, such as the kitchen. Instruct everyone that all messages, phone and other, should be placed and retrieved on this board. If you have a large family, divide the message board into sections for each name. Once a family member has retrieved his message, he is responsible for removing it.

• Create a "Family Mail Center." Use a Stackable File Sorter with a separate level for each person and one level for outgoing mail. Incoming mail can be easily separated and found by whoever it belongs to. Outgoing mail will be in one place and ready to be sent. Take turns delivering the mail to the post office or designate a family member to drop it off once or twice a week.

• Enlist family members to help serve and prepare dinner. Give everyone a specific task; chopping the veggies, preparing the salad or setting the table.

---

Great Idea from . . .
**Linda Linscott**

*I write each family member's activities on our calendar. I then use different colored highlighters to highlight each person's activities. This way, everyone knows who has what going on that day.*

*Another organizing idea that has worked great for us is giving each family member their own laundry basket. Each person is then responsible for putting their own clothes away after they are cleaned.*

Linda Linscott, Milwaukee, WI

Linda is married to Patrick. She is mother of 4 children (Daniel, Megan, Brian and Colin)

- Pre-assign after-dinner cleanup duties to each family member such as clearing the table, loading the dishwasher or taking out the trash.

- Develop a "Family Chore Chart" of routine daily chores and hang it on the fridge. It should include a list of common household chores—taking out the trash, walking the dog, dusting—along with the date due and the family member responsible for getting it done. An erasable board is a good choice, since you can then easily rotate assignments for variety. Assign tasks to each member of your family. Have them check off jobs as they are completed.

- Designate a minimum of one hour per week as "Family Only Hour." This is the perfect time to catch up with each other, conduct family meetings, play a game or plan an event. Everybody must show up and participate for this to be productive and successful.

- You and your family are not locked into watching television programs only when they're scheduled. Take advantage of the VCR. Record what you're interested in and watch these programs when convenient for you and your family. Zap through all the commercials later and save time!

- Avoid a line of family members at the bathroom every morning. Stagger the time everyone must get up by 15 minutes. You can even rotate the schedule so the same person doesn't have to get up the earliest each day.

- Enforce the "Shower on Weekdays, Baths on Weekends Law." Showering is quicker. Long, luxurious baths are made for those lazy days, when everyone is not in a rush to get to work or school.

- Get a beeper attachment for family keys. Simply clap to activate the beeper when keys have been misplaced.

- Hang an erasable Month-at-a-Glance calendar and erasable marker on the refrigerator or on a wall where they won't be missed. Have each family member jot down upcoming meetings, appointments, trips or other events. In doing so, the entire family will be well-informed and will be able to plan their schedules accordingly.

- Give a little. Get a little. If your daughter asks you to drive her to soccer practice, ask her to water the plants.

- Consolidate your activities. Pick up your son from band practice and stop at the grocery store on the way home. No sense making two trips.

- Shut off the television during dinner time and use that time more constructively. Consider having each family member share something they've learned today. Make this hour *quality time.*

*At the end of your life, you will never regret not having passed one more test, not winning one more verdict, or not closing one more deal.*

*You will regret time not spent with a husband, a wife, a friend, a child or a parent.*

Barbara Bush

# Family Chore Chart

Make copies of this page and use it as your Family Chore Chart or duplicate a similar form on your computer.

Simply fill in the chores necessary this week. If the same chores are consistent on a week to week basis, first put the chores in, then make copies, so you don't have to write the same chores in each time.

Write the responsible family member's initials next to the chore, under the correct day column.

Week of _____

| Chore | Sun | Mon | Tue | Wed | Thu | Fri | Sat |
|---|---|---|---|---|---|---|---|
| | | | (Write the person's initials below.) | | | | |
| _____ | __ | __ | __ | __ | __ | __ | __ |
| _____ | __ | __ | __ | __ | __ | __ | __ |
| _____ | __ | __ | __ | __ | __ | __ | __ |
| _____ | __ | __ | __ | __ | __ | __ | __ |
| _____ | __ | __ | __ | __ | __ | __ | __ |
| _____ | __ | __ | __ | __ | __ | __ | __ |
| _____ | __ | __ | __ | __ | __ | __ | __ |
| _____ | __ | __ | __ | __ | __ | __ | __ |
| _____ | __ | __ | __ | __ | __ | __ | __ |
| _____ | __ | __ | __ | __ | __ | __ | __ |
| _____ | __ | __ | __ | __ | __ | __ | __ |
| _____ | __ | __ | __ | __ | __ | __ | __ |
| _____ | __ | __ | __ | __ | __ | __ | __ |
| _____ | __ | __ | __ | __ | __ | __ | __ |

# Chapter 5

# Children

**D**o you ask your children to put their toys away 20 times and they still don't do it? Children can be crafty when it comes to determining how far they can push your patience. In fact, if you get agitated and decide to put their toys away for them, they'll know exactly what to do or say next time to get the same result. Pretty smart, wouldn't you say? Let's face it; give your children a choice of A) cleaning up their room or B) playing with their friends, and it is obvious which they'll choose.

When we tell children we want them to get organized, we generally mean one or more of the following:

- ✓ We want them to keep everything organized and neat.
- ✓ We want them to "do" without complaining.
- ✓ We want them to stop forgetting.
- ✓ We want them to remember, without having to be reminded.
- ✓ We want them to share in the household responsibilities.

Help your children get organized. They're living in your house under your roof and once old enough, they should have responsibilities. Secondly, if your children aren't trained to manage their time and control clutter now, they will be at a severe disadvantage when they're old enough to leave home.

As you know, children very often use every excuse and trick in the book to avoid responsibility. If you want them to learn to be accountable, it's necessary to have consequences and rewards for each task. Here are some of the excuses to be aware of:

- ✓ They say they can't remember to do what you want them to do.
- ✓ They do what you ask them to do extremely slow—enough to drive you straight up the wall!
- ✓ They leave chores and tasks incomplete, especially if they know you'll finish them.
- ✓ They fake incompetence.
- ✓ They charm you into taking away their responsibilities.
- ✓ They make excuses.

We have to use fancy footwork to get kids in order. Those methods are games, bribes, consequences, rewards; basically whatever it takes!

*I have to constantly juggle between being a wife and a mother. It's a matter of putting two different things first, simultaneously.*

Madeleine L'Engle

- Set a good example for your children by being organized yourself. When parents are not organized, kids are being sent the wrong message. Everyone must play the game for it to work.
  - Children are swayed by: 1. desire for gain (rewards) and 2. fear of loss (consequences).

  **Rewards:** Tell your children that if they do what you want them to do, within the time frame you set, you'll reward them. Maybe make their favorite meal tonight, offer to play a game with them or let them stay up a half hour later.

  **Consequences:** Tell your children that if they don't do what you want them to do, within the time frame you set, then there will be consequences. Send them to bed earlier than usual, put their toys in an out-of-reach "Holding Box" where they can't touch them for a few days or tell them they can't go out to play until the chore has been completed.

  - Play the "Round-up Game." Set a timer for 5 minutes. Then have each child grab a basket and run around picking up everything out of place. Have small prizes—ice cream, candy, stickers—depending on how much they can pick up within 5 minutes.

  - Have your children sort through their toys and give to other less fortunate children. They'll be making room for new toys, plus contributing to another child's happiness simultaneously. For every toy they give up, eliminate one of their chores for the week or bake them a batch of brownies.

  - If you have more than one child, consider the color-coding system. Choose one consistent color for each child—or have your children choose their own color if they can do so without arguing with each other. Then, whenever you buy a toothbrush, hairbrush, comb, etc., buy the designated color for each child. You'll experience less fights over what belongs to who.

- Post chore lists at eye level for kids. Have them check off each chore as they complete it. Use a washable board for the chore schedule and erasable markers.

- Ensure that your children have a place for their things—toys, clothing, books—and they know where that place is. Otherwise you're going to have to put everything back yourself.

- Teach children how to do things for themselves, but make sure you help them to succeed. For example, if you want them to set the table every night, sketch out a diagram on paper for them to follow. It will save you time, plus it will help your children learn and grow.

- Instruct your children to clean their rooms at least once a week and

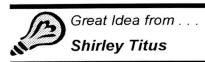

*Great Idea from . . .*
**Shirley Titus**

*I always make lunches and snacks the night before and set out clothes for the next morning.*

*It saves lots of time, especially with clothes, since the child already knows what she or he will be wearing. It stops the morning arguments!*

*Sometimes, I set up a schedule of meals for the week with breakfast included, that way I know what I'm making and do prep work the night before as well. This works out great for us!*

Shirley Titus, Pawtucket, RI
blitz192@worldnet.att.net

Shirley is married to Trent and her son's name is Kevin.

to help with dinner every night. Put this on a written schedule for them. It will help enforce the importance of responsibility.

- Ensure each child's book bag and backpack is packed with everything they need for school, day trips and other outings. Leave the bags right near the door so they're ready to go and not forgotten.

- Lower clothes closet rods to your child's eye level. This way it will be easier to get her to hang clothing up.

- Removing dozens of stuffed animals off the bed each day is time consuming for you and your children. Toy hammocks hung in children's rooms, toy chests or shelves are great for keeping the cute critters organized and out of the way.

- Instead of stacking toys in boxes, you may want to install shelves in children's rooms. Your children will more easily find what they're looking for, plus you'll prolong the life of the toys.

- Assist your children in setting up their own files. Get them brightly colored hanging file folders, along with manila files and labels. Some categories might be:
  - ✓ poetry
  - ✓ artwork
  - ✓ assorted paper
  - ✓ greeting cards from close family and friends
  - ✓ rock star photos/facts
  - ✓ blank greeting cards
  - ✓ birthdays and other events
  - ✓ stickers

- Teach them that once a file has "50" papers inside, they should first toss something out before inserting anything new—or start an additional file folder.

- See-through containers, which come in various sizes, are better than opaque ones. Children can then locate their things without having to empty each box out to find something.

- Give each of your children a handled tote bag to transport toys from one room to another or to bring with them during travel.

- Securely tape your child's signed permission slips to his schoolbooks so there's little chance they will get lost.

- To avoid a morning rush, help your children lay out tomorrow's clothes the night before. Help them assemble their entire outfit and hang it on a hook, or place it on a dressing table. This will save tons of time the next morning.

---

*If you can dream it, you can do it. Always remember that this whole thing was started by a mouse.*

Walt Disney

- Teach your child to put completed homework in her book bag, but watch her do it until she regularly does it on her own without supervision. Make her a checklist if necessary.

- Are your children always losing their gloves and mittens? Sew a long piece of yarn between each pair. Run it through their coats, inside and out both sleeves. They'll never lose them again.

- To help keep toys under control use a toy box with a lid. A closed lid means children must ask to get toys out. An open lid means they are free to take one or two toys out at a time.

- If your children refuse to organize the toy area when asked to, declare it off limits for a day or two. Enforce these measures every time you ask them to clean up and they don't.

- Use the rule of 2. Only two toys are allowed out at any one time. This will help to keep toys under control.

- Institute a "Holding Box." When a toy or another item is left out of place, take it and place it in the Holding Box. The rule: no matter what day the item went in, it must not be retrieved again for 7 days—or 5, or 3 depending on your aggravation level. If you treat this system seriously, it should work like a charm.

- Clear, shoe bags hung in a closet will store children's action figures, hair accessories, playing cards, jacks, crayons and other small items. Kids can then find what they want at a glance.

- Label each child's hat, gloves, eyeglass case and book bag with their name and address. When something is misplaced at school teachers will have the necessary information they need to return lost belongings to the appropriate student.

- Store small, easy-to-lose game pieces, toys and puzzle pieces in Zip-lock bags. Keep these bags in the game boxes.

- Buy three or four videos, books or games for your children to give as birthday gifts when they are invited to parties. Wrap, label and put them away until needed.

- If your children come home hungry after school, give them a quick, nutritious snack that doesn't require lots of cleanup. A bowl of fruit or some raw veggies and cheese are healthy choices. This is also a great time to catch up on your child's day at school, sign permission slips and review homework assignments.

- Hang a corkboard in each child's room so that he can display his drawings, favorite photographs and other papers.

- Many people are sentimental about keeping their children's artwork and toys, but it really helps to determine what, and what not, you

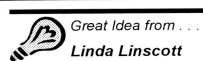

**Great Idea from . . .**

**Linda Linscott**

*I keep a file holder on the microwave. When the kids have papers they need signed, they have a place to put them. And I know where to find them.*

Linda Linscott, Milwaukee, WI

should be really sentimental about. After all, if you keep 10 things a year for 2 children for 16 years, you'll end up with 320 items!

## Young Children and Infants

- Unless young children have been playing in the mud, it may not be necessary to bathe them every night. Consider switching to every other night.

- With a baby in the house, consistent feeding times are essential. To remember to feed your baby at the same times each day, wear a watch with a timer to jog your memory.

- Pre-pack a baby bag with a blanket, diapers, moist tow-elettes, a small toy, a change of clothes, plus a list of any last minute items you may need. This way, when you have to leave with the baby, you'll be all packed and ready to go.

- When going out to a restaurant with your 1 or 2 year old, be sure to bring a fluffy toy along for her to play with—instead of noisy keys which could disturb others. You might also want to attach it to the high-chair with a piece of yarn or ribbon so that, when she tosses it, it won't go very far and you can retrieve it easily.

- If you're expecting a baby soon, make sure that the vital people—spouse, partner, other family members—can be notified quickly. If you don't already own them, you may want to rent a few beepers when the time is near.

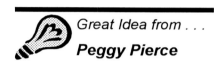

### Great Idea from . . .
### Peggy Pierce

*I'm a mother of six children and four grandchildren. When I ask the kids to pick up their toys, we make it a Counting Game. In doing so, they are learning their numbers and picking up toys the fun way.*

Peggy Pierce, Cheshire, MA

## Call the Babysitter

- Make a list of potential baby sitters with their names, addresses and phone numbers. Keep it near the phone.

- Babysitters are not just for when you're going out. If you need time with your spouse, hire a babysitter to care for young children in another room for 2 hours a night.

- Make a checklist for the babysitter. Include important instructions and phone numbers. Hang it on the refrigerator. When not in use, keep this checklist in a file for the next time you need it.

- Get together with other families and organize a Babysitting Co-op. Each family is responsible for so many hours of watching the kids.

- Get organized when you babysit. Pick up a few kid-oriented movies at the video store. Have popcorn and juice boxes on hand. Once children are pre-occupied, they will be quiet and calm, resulting in a fun night for the kids and a less stressful job for you.

# Babysitter's Checklist

Make copies of this page and use it as your Babysitter's Checklist or duplicate a similar form on your computer.

Simply fill in each line and add any special instructions. If the same instructions are consistent each time, first put the information and instructions in, then make copies, so you don't have to re-write the same notes each time.

## Our Home Information

You are at the home of_____

Our address here is_____

Location Description if Needed (e.g. next to the firehouse)_____

Our phone number here is_____

## Information on Where We Will Be

We will be at this address_____

We can be reached at this number_____

Our estimated time of return is_____

## Emergency Phone Numbers

For Emergencies **DIAL 911**

Police_____

Fire _____

        In Case of Fire:    1) Leave home immediately with all children in hand.

                               2) Call fire department from a neighbor's house.

Poison Control_____

Close friend or relative: Name _____ Number_____

## Special Instructions

1. Don't open the door to anyone unless we've given you other specific instructions.

2. Visitors Allowed? (circle one).....................................Yes...................................No

3. Keep personal phone calls to a minimum and to lengths of less than 10 minutes. We may need to reach you.

4. Children should be in bed by (circle one)...............7:00PM........8:00PM.......9:00PM.......10:00PM.......11:00PM

5. Children are allowed the following snacks:_____

6. _____

7. _____

8. _____

9. _____

10. _____

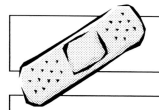

# Organizing Clinic

## Question from . . . **Julia Erickson, Forest Grove, OR**

*Q. My son, Kyle, is a sophomore in high school. I am looking for tips to share with him to help him get more orga-nized, without having to nag him. He has a student planner—but rarely uses it. We need a system. He has a lot of problems with paper and other clutter. He has a school binder with dividers, but the papers are rarely in the right sec-tions. He also does not plan out his time as far as doing assignments and tends to wait until the last minute. He gets good grades, but I know he could do better if he tried and put a little more time and effort into his work.*

(Julia, an office manager for a physician, is married to Scott, a Project Superintendent for a construction company. They have two bright children in their lives, Kyle and Bryce. They also have a very spoiled English Springer Spaniel named Mr. Rip.)

**A.** Julia, try these ideas:

### Paper clutter problem

Try ditching the school binder and working with pocket folders—one for each subject and each in a different color. You can find them at Office Max—or another office supplies store—for around $0.25 each. These folders open like a book, and have one pocket on the left and another on the right. Sometimes the middles are stapled to separate the left from the right, but I suggest the ones that are not stapled. They're easier to get papers in and out of. Clearly label the front of each pocket folder with the appropriate subject. The main purpose of using *colored* pocket folders is for your son to be able to quickly identify the appropriate school subject in the blink of an eye, without having to flip through a binder or planner to do so. Next, clearly label the inside left, and inside right of each folder:

Left = Needs to be completed      Right = Completed

When his teachers give him homework assignments and notes he must study, he should place them on the left. When he's done with homework that he must hand in, it gets placed on the right. These folders should be kept in a backpack.

### Scheduling problem

Make sure he has a Month-at-a-Glance calendar. The ones that show a day or a week at a time are not good tools for planning ahead. It's important that he can see the entire month. Each day on the calendar should be large enough to hold a number of different scenarios and maybe you could work with him to come up with a coding system. For example, if a test is coming up, he would just go to the appropriate month/day, and write "T."

Some helpful codes may be:

T = Test      D = Day Off      P = Pep Rally      H = Homework      S = Study Time      F = Final Exam

You get the idea. He'll be able to see each item that is coming up, well ahead of time.

### Motivation

Julia, your son is already getting good grades—which is excellent—so he probably doesn't really see a problem here. In order to help him get organized, you're really going to have to work with him. I'd strongly suggest a consistent, once-a-week meeting (example: Fridays at 5:00PM). You and he would meet and go through his folders. Instruct him to go through each folder, one-by-one, purging all paperwork that is completed and done with. Don't do it for him. Just sit with him, make sure he does it correctly and coach him. If a paper is in the incorrect folder, instruct him to fix it now.

The same goes for scheduling. Have him open his calendar and look at upcoming events—tests, softball games, etc. Help him determine how far ahead of time he needs to begin studying to get good grades on a particular test. Help him to schedule intervals during the week to do so.

Since he's a high school student, a small *bribe* may help immensely. Sit down with your son and come up with a reward; something really motivating, that you'll give him at the end of the school year—or at the end of each month—if he com-plies with this system consistently and if he meets with you each scheduled meeting; cash is one reward, or tickets to a ball game or telling him he doesn't have to mow the lawn.

Julia, please keep us posted on Kyle's progress.

*I never could have done what I have done without the habit of punctuality, order and diligence.*

Charles Dickens

## Chapter 6

# Students

Whether you are taking a class or your children are students in school, effective organization is essential. Homework, forms, test results, study guides and writing paper are carted around from class to class, from school to home and back. Give yourself the opportunity to be disorganized and you're, no doubt, going to lose or misplace something.

Of course, the other part of this student organization equation is effective planning. You don't want to be late for classes, scramble and cram for tests or get lower grades. With the proper precaution and a little planning, you can get and stay organized while you're being educated.

- For students, age 14 and over, student organizers or planners are essential. They're perfect for holding and categorizing tests, homework, forms, permission slips and study materials. The good ones include calendars, schedules, To Do Lists and other planning tools.

- Rather than using Day-at-a-Glance calendars, use Month-at-a-Glance instead. They should have large enough spaces to include a number of notes. Use them to plan and schedule time for assignments, homework, tests and other school-related activities.

- Instead of a spiral notebook, a 3-ring binder or pocket folders are generally the better choice for students. They're more flexible for inserting and removing handouts, notes, tests and readings.

- Don't take on more activities than you can possibly handle. Make a quick grid of the time you need for schoolwork and homework. Then fit in your extra activities around them. Be sure you include the time it will take you to get from one activity to another.

- As a general rule of thumb, you'll need at least 2 hours of study time for each hour of class time. Study time should be scheduled and written on your calendar.

- Don't cram for your tests at the last minute. Determine how many study sessions you'll need and schedule them on your calendar.

- You may consider taking a speed-reading course to get through your assignments quicker.

- The better your memory, the better your grades. There are many books for enhancing your memory. Read, practice and apply the principles so that memorization will be easier for you.

- Instead of writing and re-writing drafts of book reports or other homework, use your computer and a word processing program. It will help increase your productivity, while reducing your workload by 50% or more.

- Scheduling half-hour study sessions are generally more effective than long, marathon sessions. You'll remember more and you won't get exhausted.

- Don't leave upcoming tests, classes and other important items to your memory alone. With everything you have going on in your life, you're bound to forget something. Eliminate this possibility by always writing everything down when fresh in your mind.

- Make a Master List of everything you want to accomplish. Then, transfer those items a little at a time to your daily To Do Lists. As you complete each item, simply cross it out.

- Save the time it will take you to visit the library by making use of the available encyclopedias, dictionaries and other educational resources on the Internet instead.

- If you have a combination lock on your school locker, it may help to jot the combination down on a small piece of paper and keep it in your wallet or carrying case. You may think it is easy to remember something as simple as a combination number, but when you're in a rush or if you have something else on your mind, you may not be able to recall it quickly.

- Wake up early enough to get ready for school without rushing. If you need 45 minutes to shower, dress and have breakfast, set your alarm clock accordingly. To ensure you get up when your alarm clock goes off, put your clock on the other side of the room. This way, when the alarm sounds, you'll have to walk all the way to the other side of the room to turn it off. You're bound to *really* wake up!

- Don't leave for school at the last minute. Prepare ahead for traffic and other unforeseen circumstances that will cause you to arrive late. If it generally takes you 15 minutes to get to school, leave home at least a half hour early.

- Pre-select an outfit to wear to school the night before so you don't waste time in the morning. Put it to one side of your closet or lay it out on a dressing table.

- Don't wait until the morning rush to gather your books and school papers. Get everything ready and set to go the evening before.

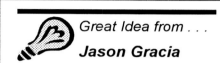

**Great Idea from . . .**
**Jason Gracia**

*Make daily To Do Lists of everything you want to accomplish in a given day. Prioritize the list so that the most important activities are always on top.*

*Whatever you didn't complete the day before should be placed at the top of the new day's list.*

Jason Gracia
Student UW-Madison
Madison, WI

**Chapter 7**

# Busting Clutter

Imagine all the possessions you and your family can accumulate over a one-year period. Maybe you don't have to imagine. Perhaps they're staring you in the face right now!

Generating clutter is a piece of cake. The larger your family, the more clutter potential you have. Whether or not it has reached the point that you're actually contemplating moving out to escape it, bringing some order back into your home will eliminate chaos and instill harmony.

Webster's Dictionary defines clutter as "an untidy mess; a state of disorder; things left around untidily."

Boy, that seems pretty mild. I'd like to add a bit to that description. It's clutter if . . .

✓   it is damaged and you have no aspirations to repair it.

✓   using it is more bother than it's worth.

✓   you never use it.

✓   you don't like it.

✓   it is obsolete.

✓   you've outgrown it physically.

✓   you've outgrown it mentally.

✓   it is too fragile or dainty to enjoy.

✓   it is too good to use.

✓   it is the wrong size.

✓   it is the wrong color.

✓   it is the wrong style.

✓   it is uncomfortable physically.

✓   it is uncomfortable mentally.

✓   it is not flattering.

✓   it makes things more difficult.

✓   it has no useful purpose.

When you come across something that meets any of the above criteria, get rid of it immediately. And if you hate the thought of throwing something out, consider donating it.

- If you own something that is *too nice to use*, it's clutter. Use it or give it to someone who will use and enjoy it.

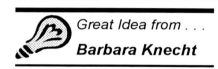

*Great Idea from . . .*
**Barbara Knecht**

*Keep everything in its selected place. After you're finished using something, put it away immediately to avoid clutter.*

Barbara Knecht, Florida, NY

Barbara is a teacher. She is married to Mike. They have a daughter, Lauren and a son, Michael. The family kitties are: Kitty, Junie, CB, Tiger, Oreo, Frankie and Daisy Mae.

- Do you save every box that comes into your possession because you might need to pack a gift *someday*? Saving three is fine, but don't save thirty-three! Of course, you may choose to eliminate them completely. When you purchase a new gift, the store clerk will, most likely, provide you with a new gift box.

- Do you have something that you don't like, but are keeping because it was given by someone special? Maybe a large number of your possessions meet this criteria. If you're not using and/or enjoying these items, they're just taking up space. Take photos of these sentimentals and save them in a scrapbook; toss the unwanted item. Keep the memory, rather than allowing the physical item to waste space.

- Keep a "Charity Box." Anytime you come across something you're no longer using, put it in this box. Visit the charity of your choice with your donations once a month or more.

- Did you or a family member do something as a hobby one time, that hasn't been touched in years? Don't let the materials clutter your home. Purge or donate half-crocheted blankets, semi-built model airplanes and partially carved wood.

- Pull out old board games taking up space and gathering dust on your shelves. Weed out the ones your family never plays with. Give them away to friends or to a charity organization.

- Schedule a consistent date every three months to get rid of expired prescriptions, medications and food items that are past their prime—throw out that green cream cheese! This is vital to the health and well-being of your family and to the happiness of your home.

- Plants need tender loving care to grow. If you don't have the time to properly care for them, get plastic ones or don't have any at all.

- Newspapers have a shelf-life of one to two days; magazines are outdated within a month. Unless you're thinking of converting your home or office into a library, throw old issues out. Your local library has plenty of back issues on file if you ever need them.

- Do you have so much in your purse that you can barely locate your wallet when you need to pay for something? In reality, you probably only need your wallet, a checkbook, a change purse, your keys and some personals. Buy a smaller purse. You won't have the opportunity to fill it with junk!

- Only keep things you can identify. Don't laugh! There are a million junk drawers out there with alien items. No one knows where they came from or what they do. If you can't identify the purpose of the item you have, it's junk. Toss it.

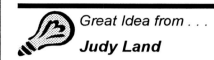

**Great Idea from . . .**
**Judy Land**

*Excluding holiday decorations and tuxedos, if you haven't used it in the last 6 months, throw it away. You probably don't need it, whatever it is.*

Judy Land, Sturgis, MI

Judy has been married to her husband, David, for 29 years.

She has 3 children (Darrin, Adrienne, and Briana) and 8 grandchildren (Erica, Myles, Collin, Logan, Mariah, Dallas, Stephanie and Paige.)

- If it disturbs you to dump things, even if you're never going to use them again, consider passing them on to someone else. Ask friends, family or associates if they want it. If not, donate it. Your local Salvation Army will probably take it if in fairly good condition.

- Avoid the "Halfway-house Syndrome." That's when you put something someplace temporarily until you decide what you're going to do with it. These temporary areas most often turn into permanent areas—better know as clutter. Force yourself to make a firm decision whether to toss or keep something. If you decide to keep it, use it. If not, get rid of it today.

- **Keep or Toss Test.** The next time you're contemplating whether or not you should Keep or Toss, use these questions to help you decide:

    ✓  Have I used this item in the past year?
    ✓  Is it serving a specific purpose?
    ✓  Do I still like it?
    ✓  Is there a legal reason for keeping it?
    ✓  Do I have a place to store it where I will find it again?

    Remember, when you keep something that no longer serves a purpose or has outlived its value or usefulness, you're wasting space, time, money and energy.

    • For items you're *truly* sentimental about, use them and enjoy them. Don't keep them boxed up in a closet.

    • Invite a friend over to help you dejunk or hire a professional organizer. Sometimes the help of another person may be all the motivation and support you need.

    • Clutter has a tendency to grow and get out of hand. Spend 15 minutes each day clearing off tabletops and desks and you won't give clutter a chance to set in.

    • Have a place for everything and always put things back where they belong when you're through using them. Using the "I'll put this back when I get a chance" technique, does not work. Put it away now and stop any chance of clutter-building.

- Hold a rummage sale. What a great way to get rid of quite a bit of clutter in one weekend!

- Is your problem paper clutter? If so, schedule a minimum of 5 minutes per evening to file the important stuff in your filing cabinet and to toss the unimportant papers out a little at a time.

- In the words of Henry David Thoreau, "Simplify. Simplify." The less you have, the less opportunity to generate clutter.

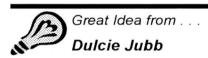
*Great Idea from . . .*
**Dulcie Jubb**

*Don't leave things just laying around where they're bound to get lost.*

*After you use something, immediately put it back when you're finished with it.*

Dulcie Jubb, St. Francis, WI

Dulcie is a proud "Aussie" originally from Perth, Australia.

## Chapter 8

# Organize for Safety

**B**etter to be safe than sorry. Here are a few things you could do to make sure you and your family are organized and prepared in any situation.

- Keep a list of Emergency Phone Numbers near the telephone. Program a few numbers directly into speed dial if your phone has this feature. Keep this list of speed dial numbers on or near the phone.

- Create a "Home Emergency Kit" and keep it in an easily accessible place, but away from the reach of young children. Include candles, matches, a flashlight, batteries, first aid kit, fuses and anything else you could think of that you might need quickly in case of a power outage or other emergency.

- Make a "Home Inventory List" of your valuables. Write down the item name, make/model and any serial numbers. Store this list in a fireproof box. While you're at it, make a copy of your driver's license and any other documents that you may need to retrieve as proof in case of a loss. Keep your list up-to-date, and you'll be totally organized when the time comes to gather any of these.

- Protect yourself by using a camcorder to document valuables in your home. Keep this video in a fireproof box, along with other inventory records including lists and photos.

- Design an "In Case of Fire Plan." Draw up a home floor plan, clearly identifying all exits. Hold practice fire drills with your family until everyone knows the procedures in case of an emergency.

- Cell phones are expensive, but when used for emergencies they can be lifesavers. Consider a separate one for each family member. Ask them to carry it with them when they go out. If you're on a budget, instruct them to use their cell phone strictly for emergencies.

- Create a "Just in Case List" so that everyone in your family is aware of solutions to potential problems. Include a checklist for things such as turning off the water shut off valve, setting the VCR or cleaning up a spill on the carpet.

- Store a flashlight in the nightstand of each family member. In case of a power outage, everyone will be prepared. You'll prevent bumps and bruises otherwise incurred by walking in the dark.

*Things which matter most must never be at the mercy of things which matter least.*

Goethe

# Chapter 9

❖❖❖❖❖❖❖❖❖❖❖❖❖❖❖❖❖

# Ideas to Hold and Store

Where the heck is that remote control? Has anyone seen my keys? Mom, where are my glasses? Sound familiar? The trick to finding what you need when you need it, is always to have a place for everything and keep everything in its place. If something doesn't have a specific home it will be misplaced. Here are some storage ideas and techniques.

Use this handy guide to determine where something should be stored:

✓ Daily Storage Areas: These areas are meant for items you use at least once a day (hairbrush, blow dryer, toothpaste, keys, razor, slippers). Store within arms reach of the place you use them.

✓ Weekly/Monthly Storage Areas: These areas are meant for items you use on a weekly or monthly basis (nail polish, biking gear, bowling bag, shoe polish). These items should be stored in easily accessible areas, which may take a minute or two to retrieve. You know—those areas that you have to bend or stretch a bit to get to.

✓ 6 Month/Annual Storage Areas: These areas are meant for items you use infrequently, such as every 6 months or annually (holiday lights, fine china, out-of-season clothing, tax returns). Store in clear, labeled, out-of-the-way containers.

• Categorize items into similar groups. Keep toys and games in one area, books and magazines in another and writing supplies in another. Use organizing containers to keep everything together, organized and easily accessible.

• Display family photographs on the wall. They'll take up less space and won't have to be moved from dressers and shelves every time you have to dust.

• Store sets in one place, such as pants that go with coordinating shirts and coffee mugs that go with matching dishes.

• For scrunchies and other circular hair ties, keep them all in one place by wrapping them around a cardboard paper towel roll.

• Stow sleds, ice skates and ski gear during the summer months.

• Stash kites, bikes and swimming apparatus in the winter.

*Great Idea from . . .*

## *Margie Pisano*

*When organizing closets and cabinets, always keep the items you use most within easy reach.*

*It shouldn't take you more than a few seconds to grab something you use on a daily basis. If it takes longer, you don't have it stored in the most effective place.*

Margie Pisano, Jersey City, NJ

Margie, my mom, is married to my dad, Mike. They have one other daughter; my sister, Jude. They also have a dog named Heidi and a cat named Luke.

- Paper towels are one of the best inventions ever. They're sanitary and they don't need to be washed. Keep them on a wall-mounted paper towel holder in the kitchen, laundry room, bathroom or anyplace else that you tend to use paper towels.

- Keep a basket with things that need to be mended or buttons that need to be secured, right near the telephone. You can easily mend something when you're talking on the phone, and accomplish two things at once.

- Consider buying a lap desk. When you're watching television or listening to music, you can bring your lapdesk to the sofa and do some light paperwork or reading in comfort. Buy one with inside compartments so that you can store items you might need right away—pens, paper clips, paper—without having to get up from your comfortable spot.

- Always put eyeglasses in an eyeglass holder or on a hanging chain around your neck. Under no circumstances should you just place them down somewhere for a minute. You're bound to spend the next hour looking for them.

- Use clear, plastic, shoebags with divided pouches for both storage and display. Those with smaller pouches can hold jewelry, safety pins and other mini items. Those with larger pouches can hold hosiery, scarves, socks, gloves and other belongings of that size. These organizers can be found in dollar stores and mail order catalogs.

- Empty film canisters, pill bottles or thermometer cases are all perfect for storing needles, pins and buttons.

- Top a round, plastic garbage can with a simple wooden circle and decorative skirted cover to make a bedside or end table. You can use it to store and conceal belongings inside, such as children's toys, pet toys, linens and more.

- When you insert multiple disks into your compact disc player, don't put the empty, plastic cases away. Stack them near your player, in the order that you put the disks in. When you're finished enjoying your music, replace the disks in each case and put everything back in the proper place.

- Store videos in an organized video holder or cabinet in the family room. Arrange alphabetically by title, or by title within genre.

- Ice cube trays and compartmentalized Appetizer Trays also double as drawer organizers for earrings, buttons, pocket change and other small trinkets.

- The Rolodex™ is not only for business. Use one at home too and

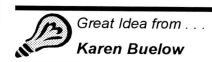

**Great Idea from . . .**
**Karen Buelow**

*I hang clear shoe organizers on the insides of doors (i.e. utility room, playroom, closets).*

*In the pockets, I put anything that used to go into junk drawers (elastics, pins, paperclips, tape) or winter supplies (hats, gloves, mittens, scarves) or summer supplies (lotion, mosquito spray, sun hats).*

Karen Buelow, Germantown, TN

Karen is a Captain with the USAF Reserves.

She's also a volunteer Coordinator for the American Institute for Foreign Study. Karen recruits host families from around the country to host students from abroad for a few months or a school year. As an incentive, she offers scholarships to families who host a student.

Interested parties can email her: D1buelow@aol.com

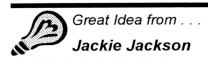

### Great Idea from . . .
### Jackie Jackson

*When tidying up after your spouse and kids, designate a "Lost Property Office."*

*I use a pretty wicker hamper for this purpose, which lives on top of the refrigerator.*

*Any stray items I find around the house, go into this hamper.*

*When someone asks, "Where is my . . .?" I direct them to the hamper.*

*Family members eventually find it easier to put their stuff away, than to search through the cluttered hamper!*

Jackie Jackson
Polar Motor Company
http://www.polarmotor.com

keep all of your associates and friends in one place for easy retrieval of phone/address information.

• Use one of your Rolodex™ cards to list the credit card numbers that you regularly use for mail order. Also indicate the expiration dates since sales clerks will generally ask for that information. By doing so, you won't have to go through your wallet and retrieve your card every time you want to order something.

• Keep it out-of-sight and out of the way. The back sides of doors are great for holding mirrors, baseball caps, small baskets and laundry bags.

• Bamboo steamers—circular, wicker baskets that stack on top of each other—can double as jewelry organizers. Keep each type of jewelry, including necklaces, bracelets, watches and rings on its own level.

• Mount a key holder near the front door. When you enter your home, put your keys on the holder. In addition, always keep an extra house key with you at all times, in your purse or wallet, in case you get locked out. Or ask someone you trust to keep an extra set for you, just in case.

• Organize your extra batteries in a battery holder, basket or tin rather than allowing them to accumulate and roll around in your drawer. If they're all kept in one place, they'll be handy when you need them.

• Shoeboxes that are in good condition make perfect storage containers. They're great for holding light bulbs, batteries, sunglasses, film and more. You can even jazz them up. Determine where you want to use the shoebox and observe the surrounding décor. Then, simply pick up some matching fabric at your local material store. Wrap the top and bottom of the box separately with the fabric. Glue the fabric on and you have your own customized storage container that is pretty enough to leave out in the open.

• Closet organizers may double or even triple your closet space. It is strongly suggested though, that you buy high-quality units and get a professional to install them for you.

• Build up, not out. Put shelves up, hang calendars and photographs on the walls and put hooks on the doors. This will help free up more storage space. Look around. Determine how much empty wall and door space you have and put it to use.

• Don't toss extra keys in a shoebox without first identifying them. A code written on a small piece of masking tape will help you find the key you need. Or dot a spot of florescent paint on the key and a dot of matching color paint on the lock, so you'll know which key goes with which lock. By the way, if you have keys to items you no longer own, throw the keys out.

- Dedicate one of your drawers a "Hobby Drawer," rather than storing everything in a thousand different places. If your hobby is one that takes up a substantial chunk of space, consider using a trunk or large plastic container to keep all of your items together, neat and organized.

- Mount a Sewing Spool/Bobbin holder to your wall for easy access to different types and colors of thread.

- Think of new uses for items you find in your house that are just taking up space. Straw baskets are not just for Easter. Use them to organize medications or bath soaps. Cloth make-up bags are perfect for holding hair accessories. A child's pencil case is great for holding spare keys.

- Corner Shelves add space to all rooms. They're perfect for holding cooking oils, knick-knacks, framed pictures, etc.

- Never put a larger item over a smaller item. For example, don't put the newspaper over the keys. This simple tip could save you hours!

- Buy holders at the hardware store for your brooms and mops, so they're not falling all over and getting in the way.

- Mount a wooden "Add-a-Drawer" under a cabinet for extra storage. These are sold by a company called *Get Organized*. You can get a free catalog by calling 1-800-803-9400.

- If you remember Fred Flintstone, you'll recall that every time he opened his closet, his bowling ball would drop on his head. Ouch! Of course, Fred recovered very quickly from this injury. You might not. So be very careful about placing heavy items on top of high shelves. In fact, don't do it. Store heavy items on the bottom to prevent any accidents.

- Magazine racks are clutter magnets. If you can't keep yours organized, buy a plastic or cardboard magazine box instead. Once it's full, you won't have the opportunity to insert another magazine in it, until you toss one out.

- Drawer organizers with individual compartments—the type that expand to fit any drawer—give you that extra needed storage space.

- Besides fishing gear, a Fishing Tackle Box—the kind that has multiple trays and sections—is perfect for holding all sorts of items, including but not limited to, sewing supplies, art supplies, buttons, beads, and more.

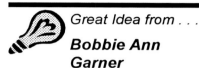

**Great Idea from . . .**
**Bobbie Ann Garner**

*I am an avid quilter and pick up fabric odds and ends everywhere I go. The hardest thing about this is "where to store it."*

*My grandfather, Owen Specht (the King of Frugal Finds) often walks the junkyard and comes home with great treats.*

*His latest find was an old baby crib. We used the two long sides and hinged them to the inside of my sewing closet door. I use the rungs as fabric hangers.*

*Not only does it keep out the clutter, but it's a great way to recycle old furniture!*

Bobbie Ann Garner, Richmond, IN

Bobbie enjoys quilting and studying child development. She is a stay-at-home mom and an Educational Consultant for:

Discovery Toys: Changing the world one child at a time

eductoys@aol.com
http://discoverytoysinc.com
420 North 21st Street
Richmond, IN 47374

# Chapter 10

# Kitchen Storage

Besides being the food preparation center, the kitchen is often the hub for other home activities. Many people use the kitchen as their main dining area. The kitchen table often doubles as the bill paying desk. This room is sometimes the family meeting room, the homework place, the call center or the event planning area.

Regardless of what you use your kitchen for, getting and keeping your kitchen organized will help keep it clutter free and in ship shape order.

- Hanging, wire baskets hold produce and more. Plus they utilize vertical space effectively. Hang them in your kitchen.

- Stacking racks work wonders in the kitchen to expand your available storage space. Buy a few so that you can stack cans, dishes, lids, wraps, bowls and more.

- Dump or donate rarely used kitchen appliances. These generally include, but are not limited to, bread machines, pasta makers, popcorn poppers, juicers, iced tea makers and ice cream makers.

- If possible and if your budget allows, steal some space from an adjacent stairwell and recess your refrigerator into the wall.

- Install under-the-counter cabinets with pull out shelves for maximum organization and accessibility.

- Place adjustable shelves inside cupboards at varying heights so that no space is wasted.

- Turn your breadbox into a lunch station. Include everything you need to make lunch for your children such as sandwich bags, twist ties, bread, snacks, lunch bags and plastic utensils. You'll get your kids out the door and off to school in a jiffy.

- Get your pots and pans out of the cabinet and hang them on an overhead rack, along a range hood or over an island. You can also purchase wall grids for this same purpose.

- Fit unused wall space with wire organizers, pegboards, dish racks or shallow open shelving. Use open areas above your cabinets for both storage and display.

- Try to choose matching appliances whenever possible. One color scheme always looks more organized.

- Is there a surplus of twist ties scattered among your drawers? Keep a maximum of five and throw the rest away. Don't worry. When you buy new garbage bags, you'll get new twist ties in the box.

- If you have an immediate use for an empty jar or container, by all means, use it. However, discard all those other jars and containers not serving any purpose and taking up valuable space.

- Use "Roll Down Can Racks" in your cabinets to hold canned vegetables, pet foods and other items in cans. When you remove a can, another rolls down. Some hold over 60 cans at once!

- Keep spices and herbs in clear, labeled bottles. If the spices are stored top view, put the labels on top; if they're stored side view, put the labels on the side. Store on a spice rack and alphabetize so they're quick and easy to find.

- Store foods bought in advance in a different storage area than the products you've already opened. Otherwise, you'll end up with 3 opened mustard jars or 2 half-used containers of milk.

- Make a bunch of "Do Not Eat!" labels—preferably on your computer. Stick a label on prepared foods you're saving for special guests or for your holiday dinner to ensure family members know they shouldn't be snacking on them.

- Store paper grocery bags that you use for garbage, right behind your garbage pail. By the way, you don't need a million of them! Five to ten should be plenty. You'll be picking up more on your next trip to the grocery store, so there's no need for a surplus.

- For food in your refrigerator and freezer, rotate oldest to the front and newest to the back. This way, the groceries you bought a while back will get used up first.

- Clear canisters can store dry foods, such as pasta and dried beans. Plus, they are decorative enough to store in plain view.

- Don't just toss your silverware in the drawer. Use silverware trays with compartments to store forks, spoons, butter knives and other everyday utensils.

- Many people store their dishes in the dishwasher. If you do too, how do you and family members know whether or not the dishes inside have been cleaned yet? A quick system is to place a magnet right side up when they're clean and upside down when the cycle hasn't been started yet. By the way, make sure your magnet can be immediately identified as right side up and upside down, so there's no confusion or question about it.

- Use a "Rolling Kitchen Island" for extra storage space. Some have flip-up cutting board table-tops for meal preparation space.

*Own less, do less, and say no.*

Geoffrey Godbey

- Label everything that goes into your freezer with a name and a date, otherwise 6 months from now, you'll be wondering what the heck is in that mysterious package. You might even be scared to open it! You can now buy freezer bags with a handy strip to write on directly, that won't rub off.

- Organize your refrigerator by foods. Here's a quick guide:

  ✓ **Top shelf:** milk, juice, soda and other beverages
  ✓ **Middle shelf:** leftovers and other prepared food
  ✓ **Bottom shelf:** unprepared food
  ✓ **Veggie drawer:** vegetables, fruits
  ✓ **Dairy drawer:** cheese, butter, spreads
  ✓ **Side door:** condiments, dressings

• Your kitchen countertop should be clean and clear. This will help keep everything sanitary and give you plenty of room for slicing, dicing and other meal preparation. Limit the items on your countertop to a few everyday appliances—microwave, toaster, coffee pot—and a container of cooking utensils.

• Wine racks display your wine bottles attractively and organize them in one place.

• Keep your everyday dishes, utensils and cooking apparatus in a convenient, easy to reach area. Other items that are only used occasionally can be placed in higher, out-of-the-way cupboards.

• Don't just keep your food wrap boxes in your cabinet in a big, disorganized pile. Install plastic wrap organizers. These can be hung discreetly inside a cabinet door.

• Leave a small jewelry box or holder—far enough away from any drains—in the kitchen. When you need to wash dishes or prepare food, you can place your rings, watches or bracelets into this box until you're done.

• For non-perishable items that you use very often, it may save you both time and money to buy in bulk.

• Organize small kitchen items—corn on the cob holders, cookie cutters, fancy toothpicks—into their own plastic, Zip-lock bags. This will help keep everything sanitary and together for easy retrieval.

- Appoint a specific "home" for each kitchen item and keep related items together. Don't store too much in any one area.

- Fancy china, glassware and utensils that are used only three or four times a year, can be stored in a place other than where the everyday dinnerware is stored. This will give you more space for your everyday dishes and glasses.

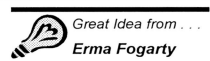

**Great Idea from . . .**

**Erma Fogarty**

*Firmly mount a long, narrow piece of wood to the kitchen wall and screw in tea cup hooks.*

*Then, instead of pots and pans taking up space and toppling in your cabinet, you can simply hang them on the hooks.*

*You could also screw these hooks under a shelf or cabinet.*

Erma Fogarty
Brown Deer, WI

Erma has 7 grandchildren, named Alissa, Ross, Brendan, Bridget, Kara, Melanie and Timothy.

- Store objects near the areas where they will be most used. Cooking utensils can be kept near the stove. Spices are usually convenient near your preparation area. Food processor blades are appropriately stored near the food processor.

- Two-tiered racks keep spices, small cans and jars at varying heights for selection at a glance.

- Separate your kitchen into imaginary quadrants:

  ✓ **Area 1:** Cooking

  ✓ **Area 2:** Preparing (chopping, slicing, dicing, coring)

  ✓ **Area 3:** Holding (keeping food warm, cooling, rising)

  ✓ **Area 4:** Cleaning

- Never overload your refrigerator. Keeping enough space around each food item will make it easier to find what you're looking for. In addition, leftovers, which must be eaten within a few days, will not be overlooked.

- Don't store anything on top of the refrigerator unless it is in an organizing container or basket. Loose items on top are liable to fall behind the fridge—not to be seen again for years.

- If you pay your bills in the kitchen, keep your bill paying supplies—check book, pen, calculator, envelopes, stamps, mailing labels—in a closed, portable container. This will help keep everything together, plus it can be stored out of the way when not in use.

- The kitchen refrigerator is a great place for a Family Message Center, Chore Chart or Grocery List. However, it's not the best place to display children's artwork, school work or certificates. Rather than the kitchen, install a bulletin board in the children's bedrooms for their artwork and other documents they're proud of.

- Store your everyday cooking utensils in an open plastic container or in a cooking utensil organizer designed specifically for this purpose, so you don't have to rummage through a drawer.

- Don't overload the surface of your refrigerator with coupons, Post-it™ notes, business cards and magnets. Once too much is attached, you won't be able to find anything.

- "Under Counter Dispensers," that dispense items such as plates, napkins, cups and coffee filters, eliminate cabinet and countertop clutter.

- Two-tiered Lazy Susans are perfect for storing canned goods, spices, extracts, dressings and condiments. Just spin this organizer until you find what you're looking for.

- Install an adjustable door rack on the back of a pantry door to store everything from soup cans to cereal out of the way, but still handy.

- Lid organizers, mounted on walls or inside cabinets, keep pot and pan lids organized and easily accessible.

*Nothing great was ever achieved without enthusiasm.*

George Ellis

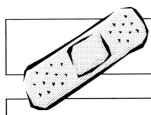

# Organizing Clinic

Question from . . . **Tina Haughenberry, Hurst TX**

**Q.** *I am a single parent of 5 beautiful animals—2 dogs (Shasha and Seca) and 3 cats (Vali, Forbes and Morgan.)*

*My problem is that I own a 4 bedroom/2 living area home with a huge open kitchen. After living here for 12 years I have accumulated tons of stuff in every room that I do not need or want. I don't know where to begin. I feel overwhelmed!*

*How can I find the motivation to clear out the unwanted things? I have thought about packing everything up like I was going to move and then unpack in my new, old house. Any suggestions?*

**A.** Tina, it seems that one of the main reasons you feel overwhelmed is because you're looking at this task as *one huge task* to tackle at once.

I suggest you start on a smaller scale. Instead of starting with the *entire house*, commit to starting with *one room*.

Just the fact that you're aware that you have stuff that you "no longer need or want" is a giant step in the right direction. That fact alone will make the task easier.

Here are some guidelines for you to follow:

[1]    Choose *one* room to start on. Write it at the top of an 8 1/2" x 11" sheet of paper. This is your *Action Sheet*.

**Example: BEDROOM A**

[2]    Designate an appropriate reward to give yourself on the "dumping portion" of the job. The *reward* concept serves as your motivation, so be sure to choose something that you'd really enjoy! Write it on your Action Sheet.

**Example: Treat yourself to a massage, go out for a nice dinner, sit by the pool for the afternoon.**

[3]    Set a specific "Dumping Completion Deadline" for this one room. Write it on your Action Sheet.

**Example: DUMPING DEADLINE: APRIL 30**

[4]    Schedule 3 specific dumping dates (one hour for each.)  Hopefully this will be enough time to complete the *dumping portion* of the job. Write it on your Action Sheet. Post your Action Sheet in a prominent place where you are certain to see it every day, like your bathroom mirror. It will serve as a reminder of your goal, deadline and pending reward.

**Example: DUMPING DATES: APRIL 18 from 8-9A, APRIL 21 from 8-9A, APRIL 24 from 8-9A**

[5]    When the first dumping day arrives, keep that appointment, just as you would any other *important* appointment. Bring a bunch of *large* garbage bags. Play your favorite music in the background.

[6]    Set a timer with an alarm for one hour.

[7]    Pick up one item at a time and start dumping. If you come across items you want to give to charity, designate a special bag for those things. Whatever you are going to keep, just put to one side of the room.

[8]    Continue doing this until the timer goes off. If you prefer to continue, fine. Otherwise, stop and follow the same procedures for your next two scheduled dates. Don't let the garbage bags sit there. Make sure they are thrown out now or on Garbage Day at the latest. Bring all donations to a local charity.

[9]    Once you've managed to dump everything you don't want or need in that one room, it's time to celebrate. Take advantage of that reward you designated.

[10]    You're ready to begin putting everything you are keeping, back in an organized manner. Be very careful from now on not to put anything else in this room that you don't need or want.

[11]    Repeat this process for each of the other rooms in your house.

Tina, please keep us abreast of your accomplishments. Good luck!

# Chapter 11

# Bedroom Storage

Do you have to stumble through an obstacle course in your bedroom? Are you scared stiff to look in your closet or under your bed? If so, this is the perfect time to initiate that needed tranquility. The bedroom is our place of rest. The surroundings should be serene, comforting and conducive to a good night's rest.

- Make your bed right after you get up in the morning. It only takes a minute and will look inviting when it's time to go to sleep again that night. Plus, it gives your bedroom a fresh, organized appearance.

- Keep matching bed linens together and store them in an area near the beds in a bedroom drawer, chest or linen closet.

- Use under-the-bed storage organizers to store blankets and out-of-season sweaters. Or purchase a bed with built-in drawers!

- Underbed storage is great for containers holding out-of-season sweaters or blankets. However, don't, under any circumstances, store *junk* under your bed.

- The only reading material on your bedroom nightstand should be the book or magazine you're reading right now. Store all other reading material back in a bookcase or rack.

- Decorator bed pillows may look nice, but are they worth the time it takes to pull them off at night and put them back on in the morning, every morning, every single day of your life? Consider simplifying by taking the pillows off.

- Appoint a specific "home" for each bedroom item. Something that doesn't have a designated spot gets lost quickly. For instance, if you designate your large jewelry box the home of your watch, it should be there ready for you to use every day.

- Declare everyone in charge of his or her own room, bed, closets and drawers. If two or more people share a room, divide and make a list of the individual responsibilities.

- If you have more than one child, invest in loft beds. You can then fit a dresser, desk or other necessary piece of furniture.

- Clear your bedroom dresser of excess colognes and perfumes. Keep the one or two that you really like and toss out the rest. A silver serving tray on your dresser nicely holds your favorite fragrances.

*Small rooms of dwelling
set the mind
in the right path,
large ones cause it
to go astray.*

Leonardo da Vinci

# Chapter 12

❖❖❖❖❖❖❖❖❖❖❖❖❖❖❖❖

# Clothes Closet
# and Dresser Drawers

Many people go through great pains to hide the interiors of their bedroom closets from others. Closets, since they are rarely thought of as a room, get little respect. Hangers are jutting up into the air. Clothes are tossed on the floor. Shoes are sprawled all over the place.

"Nobody will ever see it anyway" is expressed by millions every day.

However, that statement is simply not true. *You* see it every day. Start off each morning looking at chaos and your day will be chaotic.

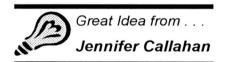

## Great Idea from . . .
### *Jennifer Callahan*

*Every time I buy new clothing, I take the exact number or more, of my old, worn out items and get rid of them. This saves on the clothing clutter a bit.*

*For instance, if I bring home 6 new pairs of socks, I go through my socks and take out at least 6 old pairs. If I bring home 3 new shirts . . . out go 3 old, worn out, or wrong sized shirts!*

Jennifer Callahan, Navarre, FL

Jennifer is married to James and is mother to Kayla, Spencer and Mckenzie.

- In order to really reorganize your bedroom closet, the best thing to do is empty it out completely. Then, carefully make a decision whether to keep or dump each item. If you haven't worn it in a year, chances are good that you'll never wear it again. Get rid of it. Dump it or donate it.

- If your budget allows, consider a custom closet organization system to keep your clothing, shoes, handbags, ties, scarves and briefcases stored in a neat and organized fashion. These systems are a bit tricky, so unless you've done it before, have it installed by a professional. You'll save yourself a headache.

- Plan to clean out and organize your closets twice a year; once in the spring, once in the fall.

- Take a survey of your closets and drawers before you go shopping for more. Don't buy more unless you:
  ✓ *really* need it and
  ✓ have a place for it.

- Consistency is imperative to good organization. First, organize your closet by articles of clothing; all of your jeans in one section, all of your blazers in another and all of your shoes in another. Then, color code within those groups.

- Buy space-saver hangers that hold 5-6 skirts vertically. They take up less room and keep your skirts in one area.

- Get shoe racks for family members to keep in their closet. Count the shoes first, leaving room for some additional pairs. Then, measure the available space—width and height. There are many shoe rack designs to choose from. In fact, I bought a nice one for less than $20 that is expandable. Shoe bags that hang on the closet door are not recommended. They're not the best for hygiene since they accumulate dirt. They're also extremely clumsy.

- If you have limited closet space, you may want to consider separating your clothing by season. You can always store the out-of-season clothing in snap-shut plastic boxes. Label the boxes with the person's name and season. Then, when the new season arrives, take a few hours to make the switch.

- When you take a hanging item out of your closet, don't leave the hanger in the original spot. When clothes are moved back and forth, it is then difficult to see the hanger. Place the empty hangers on one side of the closet to keep them neat and accessible.

- Using thin, wire hangers is not a good way to keep a closet organized. These hangers tend to twist, bend, tangle and stick up in the air. Thick plastic hangers for your shirts and blazers and quality metal clip hangers for your skirts and pants are recommended.

- Double, triple or quadruple your closet space with hangers that hold up to 12 garments at a time. Just hook one over the closet bar, hang your clothing, lift both hanger arms up and lock into place.

- Hang all articles of clothing facing the same direction for a nice, uniform look. The same goes for hangers.

- Keep only three to four extra hangers in the closet. You don't need a surplus of *eighty-seven*!

- Over the door, clear shoe bags are wonderful for holding light items such as hosiery, socks and handkerchiefs.

- Ties and belts stored in drawers are difficult to find and take up unnecessary space. Use tie and belt racks in your closet.

- When you get home from the dry cleaners, immediately take the twist tie off the batch of clothing and remove the plastic covering, unless you're not planning to wear a particular outfit for the next 6 months. Replace wire hangers with sturdy, plastic ones immediately —your dry cleaner may even take the hangers back from you if you offer. Take the time to organize your clothes immediately, or you're bound to get frustrated during the morning rush when you're looking for something to wear.

- Who says you can have only one clothing rod? Install two or three at varying heights to utilize all your hanging storage space. Be sure, however, that your clothes are not overlapping or hanging too low. For instance, you wouldn't want to hang pants on a top rod if they're covering your shirts on the lower rod. You also don't want

*True elegance consists not in having a closet bursting with clothes, but rather in having a few well-chosen numbers in which one feels totally at ease.*

Coco Chanel

clothing dragging on the floor. But, hanging shirts on a top rod and skirts on a lower rod usually works beautifully.

- Donate outgrown or unwanted clothing to charity or a resale shop. If you're never going to wear it again, it's likely to end up in the back of your closet.

- There should never be clothes on the closet floor. Hang them up, put on a shelf or fold them and put in your dresser.

- Hang a laundry bag on a hook inside the closet for clothes that need to go to the dry cleaners. When it's full, you can just grab it and bring it to be cleaned.

- Store sweaters in see-through bins underneath your bed during the warmer season.

- Keep necklaces and bracelets untangled and easily accessible by hanging them on hooks inside your bedroom closet or on a hanging jewelry organizer. Keep earrings together by using an earring tree or an ice cube tray in your drawer.

- Drawer dividers in bedroom dressers keep socks, underwear and lingerie neat and easy to find quickly. Rotate newest washed items to the back and pull previously washed items forward.

- If you don't have a legitimate use for those odd socks you're keeping in your bedroom dresser—you know, the ones that are missing their mates—get rid of them.

- Sometimes you can easily slip a chest of drawers or bedroom dresser that's taking up too much bedroom space, right into your clothes closet. This is especially nice if you have a piece that doesn't match well with your other bedroom furniture.

- If your clothes closet looks like an earthquake recently hit, limit the number of pants, skirts, shirts, shorts and jackets that you have at any given time. Eliminate something before buying something new. Quality is important; quantity isn't.

- Plan ahead and determine what you need before you go shopping. For instance, if you have a pair of gray, woolen pants but no shirt to match, indicate this on your shopping list.

- Schedule a monthly "Clothes Toss" date with those family members that have overloaded, cluttered closets and dresser drawers. Everyone should bring at least one item of clothing they hate, will no longer wear, that no longer fits or is worn out.

- Use a mesh laundry bag to toss dirty stockings and delicates in immediately. When there are enough items inside, you can just toss the entire bag in the wash.

*Have nothing in your house that you do not know to be useful or believe to be beautiful.*

Henry David Thoreau

# Chapter 13

# Living Room and Family Room Storage

The Living Room and Family Room are your home retreats meant for comfort and relaxation. After a hard day of work, it's nice to enjoy a few moments of solitude. With this in mind, we must ensure the atmosphere matches the intention.

Magazines stuffed into magazine racks and on coffee tables, books and clothing on the floor and lost remote controls instill chaos—not fun. Here are a few ideas to help transform that chaos into order.

- Never keep more than three items on your coffee table or it will become a *clutter table*. Try nothing more than a magazine, a remote control and a coffee table book.

- End tables are clutter magnets and take up space. You'll probably agree that it's easy to just walk by and place something on top of them. Replace end tables with floor lamps and overhead lighting.

- Empty out those magazine racks. A few current magazines are great for reading enjoyment. Anything more is just clutter.

- There should never be anything on the floor of the family room, except for the furniture, of course. Toys should be in a toy chest or on a shelf. Books go on the bookshelf. CDs belong in a CD Holder. Jackets and coats belong in the closet. Hats belong on the hat rack.

- Always have a specific place for the remote control and it won't get lost. Get compartmentalized pockets you can buy that hang over the arm of a sofa or armchair. They have sections to hold the remote control and the *TV Guide*. What a handy idea!

- Don't accumulate old newspapers in your magazine rack or on your coffee table. Keep today's issue. Recycle the rest.

- Hang up framed pictures to free up space. Plus there will be less to move when you're cleaning up.

- Use the type of game tables that fold-up when not in use. The same goes for snack tables.

- It's perfectly fine to keep your sewing supplies or hobby materials in the family room. That is, as long as they're in an organizing container and not spread out all over the place.

*The time to relax is when you don't have time for it.*

Sydney Harris

# Chapter 14

## Bathroom Storage

*It's the little things that drive you crazy; the broken heel, the stain, the drip. If you take care of little things, the big things become manageable.*

Heloise

Take a look through the catalogs of large department stores, such as JC Penney or Sears. Turn to the appropriate section and you'll see the ultimate bathrooms. Don't they look beautiful? There's not a thing out of place.

You might be saying, "*Well, it really doesn't look lived in.*" That phrase always makes me laugh. The reason that it doesn't look lived-in is because there's *no clutter.*

The bathroom is one of the first rooms we see in the morning, after waking up. It's the starting point for our daily activities.

Start your day off on a chaotic, cluttered note and your stress level is going to go in the wrong direction. Up!

- Go through your medicine cabinet. Toss old makeup, perfumes, toiletries and prescriptions. Dump anything with an expired date, cosmetics over a year old and anything else you no longer use.

- Always keep toothbrushes in toothbrush holders. Each family member should have a different colored toothbrush for quick and easy identification.

- Use a shower caddy for convenient access to soaps, lotions, pumice stones, shampoo, conditioner, razors, or anything else that your family uses in the shower.

- Short on cabinet space? For that extra needed storage, install shelves on the bathroom walls.

- Hanging wire fruit baskets, usually used in the kitchen, double as bathroom holders for curlers, combs and more.

- A long magnet, attached to the back of your medicine chest will hold tweezers, shavers, clippers, scissors and other metal objects neatly in place.

- If your cabinets are small, use an over-the-toilet organizer, a shelf or a wicker basket to hold powders, sprays and other essentials.

- For large bathrooms, consider putting a matching coat rack inside. It's perfect for holding robes or towels.

- A three-tiered plate rack is convenient for holding soaps, nail polish, hairbrushes, barrettes and other small items.

- Soap dispensers are generally neater and more sanitary than soap bars. You can even buy multi-pour dispensers that can be mounted to the tile and filled with your favorite soaps, lotions and shampoos.

- Assign each family member their own basket or tote bag for their bathroom personals. Hang each on a separate hook. This will eliminate confusion over what belongs to who.

- If your hair dryer has a loop, a simple nail or hook will allow you to hang it on the side of a cabinet or on the wall.

- Designate a specific *home* for each bathroom item. Don't clutter one area with too many things. Leave sufficient space around each item so you can find what you need in a matter of seconds.

- Consider using clear, organizing caddies to store similar items together. All your lotions can go in one, hair products in another and colognes in another.

- Store toiletries and paper products bought in advance in a different storage area than the products you've already opened. Otherwise, you'll have 3 half-used hair spray cans or 2 slightly finished boxes of tissues.

- Toss out stringy, ripped, faded, thinned-out bath towels. Forget the "what if I need extra rags" syndrome.

- Store bath toys in a wicker basket right near the bathtub. Toys will dry out quickly and will be easily accessible for your children.

- Catch up on the news without wasting time. Put a waterproof radio in the bathroom and listen while getting ready to start your day.

- Hang a plastic, toilet paper rack inside your under-the-sink cabinet or the back of the cabinet door. These organize and store three to four extra rolls of toilet paper.

- While watching television, I saw a home decorator sew colorful cloth pockets and then attach them to the outside of a child's shower curtain. She even spruced them up with some big decorative buttons. In one pocket, she placed hair ties, in another she put a hairbrush, another combs and so on. It looked really cute and was a great storage solution. Just be sure you have a sturdy shower rod and that you don't put anything extra heavy in the pockets.

- Keep reading clutter off the floor by installing an acrylic magazine rack to the wall or the commode to hold magazines for the entire family.

- Family members keep forgetting to put down the toilet seat? The "Self-Closing Toilet Seat" never forgets. Its automatic closing system begins lowering the seat a few minutes after use.

*Live simply
so that others may
simply live.*
Ghandi

**Chapter 15**

# Basement and Garage Storage

The basement and garage are the perfect rooms for storing things you'd rather not have hanging around in your main living quarters. Some regulars are tools, bikes, swimming pool supplies, storage containers and garden supplies.

However, these storage rooms really don't get the respect they deserve. Frequently, in fact, they are abused. Since we generally don't bring guests into them, they are given less thought and less care than other areas of the house. The only things that should be in storage are those items that you use and/or enjoy. If you have something that has generated an inch or more of dust, it's probably safe to assume it is clutter. The storage in your basement and garage must be neat and organized to be considered *storage* and not *clutter*. If you can't find it, or you can't get to it, it's clutter.

- Hang tool boards with latches for keeping long handled tools organized. Use hooks for hanging bikes and tool pegboards.

- Use a tall trashcan or umbrella stand for holding tall items such as, fishing rods, pool cues and baseball bats.

- Bikes can be stored neatly and out of the way on bike racks.

- Get rid of anything in your basement that has not been used for months. Check with your local fire department to find out how to dispose of flammable items.

- Avoid saving excess boxes in the basement. Keep one or two and throw the rest out.

- Hang a wraparound cloth apron with pockets and you'll have an instant tool tote. Make your own or purchase an inexpensive one from a home improvement center.

- Vertically mount a cardboard paper towel roll on the wall or inside a cabinet door. Use it to hold large, circular rolls of tape.

- Use a toolbox with sections so that you can divide and separate tools into their own divisions. This will make it easier to find one when you need it.

- If you live alone and your basement or garage is really going to be a bear to clean, consider hiring a high school or college student to help you out.

*Take a little time
to do it now,
or take a lot of time
to do it later.*

Anonymous

- Keep various labeled jars for nails, screws and washers. Nail or screw the cap of the jar to the underside of a board. The jars will always be in one place and you can simply unscrew the jar, take out what you need and replace it again on its mounted lid when you're finished getting what you need.

- Get a free-standing "Sports Organizer Rack" to keep equipment from soccer balls and baseball mitts to golf shoes ready for play. These steel racks have roomy shelves and hanging hooks to keep gear organized.

- If you keep your garden hose in the garage, don't just leave it tossed on the floor. Wrap it around a "Garden Hose Holder" that is mounted to the wall.

- Clear, labeled, organizing containers are perfect for the basement and garage. Store car care products in one. Store paint brushes in another. You get the picture. They will keep everything free of dust and organized for easy retrieval.

- Ensure there is sufficient lighting in your basement and garage, especially inside any closets or cabinets. Generating clutter is easy when you can't see what you're putting in or taking out.

- Don't make your basement or garage the *catch-all area* for things you don't even use. If you're storing something that is not useful or that you don't enjoy, throw it out today.

- Store weed killer, paint and other toxic materials on high shelves, out of the reach of young children.

- Keep a step-stool or step-ladder handy. You'll be able to easily reach items on high shelves. Be sure you store it in a place where young children cannot climb up.

- Create a "Pick up at the Hardware Store" list. Include items you buy at the hardware store. Make copies of this list. Hang one up in the garage or basement. Keep the rest in a file until you need a new one. As you run out of something, simply check off what you need and bring this list to the store when you go.

- Hang a tennis ball from the ceiling so it taps your car window when you've pulled in far enough. You'll prevent bumps and scratches.

- Use utility shelves in your basement storage area to hold items ranging from paint cans and garden supplies to car care products.

- After you give your basement and garage an organizing overhaul, designate 15 minutes a week to tidy up. This way, you won't have to ever waste hours cleaning them up again.

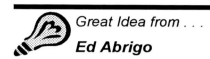

*Great Idea from . . .*
**Ed Abrigo**

*Hang each tool in your garage or basement on a pegboard. Trace around each tool with a pencil. Then, remove the tool and paint the penciled line, so that you end up with the outline of your hammer, screwdriver, saw, etc.*

*Now, your family members will know exactly where to return each tool after using.*

Ed Abrigo, Jersey City, NJ

Ed is a staff member of St. Francis Hospital in Jersey City, NJ.

# Chapter 16

# Lawn and Garden

If you have a green thumb, a lawn or garden can certainly bring you hours of enjoyment. Beautiful, weed-free, green grass is a sight to be seen. Fragrant flowers coloring your yard and homegrown vegetables waiting to be savored are such comforting thoughts. To get the best results and the full enjoyment out of your lawn and garden, a little bit of planning goes a long way.

- Plan your garden in the winter. Measure it. Sketch it out on paper. Then, when spring arrives, you'll be ready.

- Do some research before planting your garden. Determine what plants and flowers look best together. Find out where you can purchase your plants and seeds at the best value.

- Schedule time each week—or more if necessary—to take care of your garden before weeds add to your work.

- If you love fresh vegetables and you love gardening, planting veggies could save you trips back and forth to the supermarket.

- Recruit family members to help. If everyone has a particular duty they're responsible for, the job can get done quicker and everyone can reap the rewards of his or her accomplishments.

- Attend garden shows for time-saving tools, ideas and tips.

- Rather than watering your lawn manually, invest a little bit of money in an automatic sprinkler system. Put it on automatic pilot, while you rest in your hammock sipping lemonade.

- If your budget allows, a gas powered mower, rather than a manual one, will help get the job done quicker and with less exhaustion.

- Don't waste time with old, rusted, outdated tools that are hindering you from getting the job done, rather than helping you.

- Keep your garden tools in an upright tool container with slots to keep each tool organized and handy when you need it.

- Set up a written schedule of garden chores so you don't forget to do what you have to, when you have to.

- Get someone else to mow the lawn. According to a Gallup Survey, more than 22 million households a year hire professional landscape, lawn care and tree care services.

*A garden is a lot like life.*

*Neglect the little things and it will deteriorate into chaos.*

*Tend to the little things and it will thrive and become a thing of beauty.*

Joe Gracia

# Chapter 17

# Coupons

Sharing bagels and coffee with my husband while reading the Sunday newspaper is one of my favorite activities. I believe the simple things in life make it all worthwhile. During this time, I clip grocery coupons; probably over 20 a week. They're really a money-saver. My savings run anywhere from $20 to $25 per shopping trip.

However, I clip grocery coupons *because I use grocery coupons on a regular basis*. If you don't, you shouldn't be clipping them in the first place. Why? Because coupons that sit and clutter up your drawers are a waste of your time and are of no use to you.

- If you have a disorganized drawer full of coupons, immediately dump the entire thing in your trashcan. Get rid of the old. Start from scratch.

- Prior to clipping a coupon, glance at the expiration date. If you're most likely going to need that product by that expiration date, clip it and store in your coupon organizer. If not, don't waste your time clipping it.

- Each week, go through your current coupon file, for duplicate product deals. Beware of clipping doubles and triples of each product, unless you know for sure that you're going to use all of them.

- Clip grocery coupons only if you use them *consistently* on your visits to the supermarket. Keep them in a coupon organizer by category. Or get a small expandable file with 16 divisions, and create one yourself. Here are some categories:
    - ✓ *Baking/Baked Goods*
    - ✓ *Canned/Jar Goods*
    - ✓ *Cleaning/Laundry*
    - ✓ *Dairy*
    - ✓ *Meat/Fish/Poultry*
    - ✓ *Pasta/Rice/Mixes*
    - ✓ *Snacks/Candy*
    - ✓ *Baby and Pet Products*
    - ✓ *Beverages*
    - ✓ *Cereal/Bread/Breakfast*
    - ✓ *Condiments/Dressings*
    - ✓ *Frozen Food*
    - ✓ *Paper Products*
    - ✓ *Personal Care/Medications*
    - ✓ *Vegetables/Fruit*
    - ✓ *Miscellaneous*

- When you're making out your grocery list, keep your coupon organizer nearby. Pull out only those coupons you need, put them in an envelope and bring the envelope to the store with you.

- Try to plan your meals and grocery list based on the coupons you have. You'll ensure that the coupons are used before they expire.

*If you don't run your own life, somebody else will.*

John Atkinson

## Chapter 18

❖❖❖❖❖❖❖❖❖❖❖❖❖❖❖❖

# Shopping and Errands

Shopping can be fun, productive and exhilarating or it can be a totally stressful event. It's really up to you what you want your shopping experience to be.

The secret word is . . . *plan.* What are some of the benefits? You won't waste endless hours going in circles to find the perfect gift. You won't go over budget. Long lines won't be a problem. You won't forget what you meant to pick up in the first place. You'll complete the activity on a positive, uplifting note. Sound good? Read on.

- Before you go grocery shopping, look through your fridge. Discard any stale food. Clean shelves with a damp cloth. When you get back from shopping, the new groceries can go right in.

- Try to go to the supermarket during slow periods—late at night or early in the morning—when lines are short and parking isn't a hassle. If you have lots of room for storage, consider purchasing paper items, cereals and cleaning supplies in bulk to save unnecessary trips back and forth to the store.

- Create a "Master Grocery List."

    [1] Type or write up a list of groceries that you regularly pick up at the supermarket. Do this on your computer if you own one.

    [2] Once your list is complete, print it out and make copies.

    [3] Keep one posted conveniently on the refrigerator, attached with a magnet; keep the extras in a file folder labeled "Grocery Lists" so you know where they are when you need a fresh one.

    [4] Every time you, or another family member, see something running out, simply check it off on your list.

    [5] Bring your list to the market and cross out each item as you put it in your shopping cart.

- Shop in a shopping center where you can consolidate many of your errands—Dry Cleaner, Post Office, ATM, Grocery Store—into one trip. You won't be spending hours driving around town.

- When you come home from grocery shopping, put items that need to be cooled right by the refrigerator. Then, put all these items into the refrigerator at once. This will save time and electricity.

- Plan your meals before writing up your shopping list. It will be easier for you to write up your list. In addition, you won't spend money on groceries that you don't really need this week.

- When you run errands, don't leave the house without a list telling you where you need to go and what you have to get. Take your lists into each store and check off items as you go.

- Make a list of errands you regularly tend to, along with items you must bring with you when you go. For instance, list clothes for the dry cleaner, bank deposit slips for the bank, car keys, checkbook for payments and any other applicable items.

- When you run errands, don't run in circles. Start with the errand farthest from home and work your way back.

- Call ahead when you run errands. Before you make the trip, call the library to be sure the book you need is in or the video store to see if the tape you want is available. If possible, you can request that your purchase be left at the counter so you can walk in, pay and leave. A few minutes on the phone can save you an hour or more.

- Tired of driving all the way to the store, just to find out the store is out of the size jeans you wanted? What a waste of time! Consider shopping by catalog or on the web.

- Make a list of what you need before you go shopping. If you're going to a mall, indicate the exact stores you'll be stopping at and why. You'll get your shopping done in a jiffy, stress-free and without spending extra dough!

- Don't shop on the busiest days of the week. Saturday afternoons and days before holidays fall into this category. You'll spend a lot of unnecessary time getting from store to store, waiting in line and discovering what you're looking for is out of stock. Shop early in the morning, at night or far in advance of major holidays.

- Malls are getting larger and larger. With big malls come big parking lots. With big parking lots comes the possibility that you won't be able to remember where you parked your car. Always note the number of your parking spot or parking area name on an index card and keep it inside your wallet, purse or shirt pocket. If the parking lot doesn't post where you are, determine where you are parked in proximity to where the mall entrance is.

- As soon as you walk in the mall, make a written note of what store you see. This way, when you're done shopping, you can glance at your note and determine what entrance you came in. This will make it much easier to locate your automobile later.

*Always leave enough time in your life to do something that makes you happy, satisfied, even joyous.*

*That has more of an effect on economic well-being than any other single factor.*

Paul Hawken

# Grocery List

Make copies of this page and use it as your Grocery List or duplicate a similar form on your computer.

Leave this list on the refrigerator for you and your family to jot down needed groceries. Then, bring the list to the grocery store with you when you go shopping. Cross out each item as you place it in your shopping cart.

| Baking/Baked Goods | Beverages |
|---|---|
| | |

| Canned/Jar Goods | Cereal/Bread/Breakfast |
|---|---|
| | |

| Cleaning/Laundry | Condiments/Dressings |
|---|---|
| | |

| Dairy | Frozen Foods |
|---|---|
| | |

| Meat/Fish/Poultry | Paper Products |
|---|---|
| | |

| Pasta/Rice/Mixes | Personal Care/ Medications |
|---|---|
| | |

| Snacks/Candy | Vegetables/Fruits |
|---|---|
| | |

| Baby and Pet Products | Miscellaneous |
|---|---|
| | |

# Chapter 19

# Cooking

W hat's for dinner tonight? Are you planning to whip up a homemade meal or will it be takeout? If you immediately answered "take out," you probably don't spend too much time every day slaving over a hot stove.

However, for the time that you do spend cooking, good organization is a major plus in the kitchen. It can help save time, money and stress.

- Keep a half-cup measuring cup in both your flour and sugar canisters. You can scoop and measure at the same time.

- Keep a stack of inexpensive paper plates right near the microwave to use as lids when microwaving. They'll prevent splatter and cover food better than paper towels.

- Make sure you have a good set of knives to chop and dice. Over 25% of your time could be wasted using the wrong or dull knives.

- Get yourself a good set of tools to grate, peel, dice, core, puree—you get the point. There's no sense spending time struggling with poor equipment.

- Once or twice a month, treat your family to take-out food and use paper dishes and cups. You will get a day off from cooking and cleaning. Keep take-out menus handy right near the telephone.

- Wear an apron with a pocket. It will protect your clothing and keep small items handy, like a pen and paper.

- There is an overwhelming selection of pre-cut, de-boned and de-shelled items in your supermarket. They may cost a little more, but if you're not on a strict budget, the time you save will be well worth it.

- Use cooking spray on your pots and pans so that foods come off quickly, without extra effort.

- When peeling vegetables, place a plastic grocery bag on the counter so that it's open, like a cave. Peel veggies in the bag and throw the bag away.

- Keep the kitchen wastebasket right where you're preparing food. This way, when you open a box or bag that you can

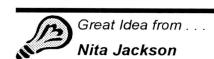

**Great Idea from . . .**
**Nita Jackson**

*I am handicapped from a car wreck and am in pain 24 hours a day. I need to cut corners every place I can to stay organized.*

*First of all we eat a lot of soup. Never be ashamed to serve soup and sandwiches!*

*And thank the Lord for that bagged lettuce!*

*With these few things, you'll have a complete meal that's fairly simple for children to make for themselves.*

*They think they are so grown up helping mommy make dinner!"*

Nita Jackson
Brightly@bigfoot.com

Organize Wize
http://organizewize.hypermart.net/

Tools, tips, timesavers and books for the busy and those longing to be organized.

*Great Idea from . . .*

### Chantal Newberry

*My fiancée and I work full time. We both go to school part time and are generally very busy people. He likes to eat like there's no tomorrow and I want to make sure we're not copping out on our budget by eating out for convenience sake!*

*So, when we do have some time (i.e. Sunday afternoon, evening), we try to make one or two big items, such as lasagna, beef stew or coq au vin. The lifesaver for these is a crock pot. Soups, stews and other yummy food can be pre-made and then frozen in individual portions.*

*When he gets home from school at 10:00PM and wants to eat something, we pop one of the portions into the microwave, warm up some fresh bread that one of us picked up on the way home and, finally, warm up a side veggie. You've got a hot meal fit for a king. Of course, some quick dessert selections of ours are Jell-O or ice cream.*

Chantal Newberry
North York
Ontario, Canada

toss, you will immediately do so. This will help keep the work area clean and you'll waste less time moving unnecessary items out of the way.

• Plan your meals with the following criteria in mind:

✓ Should be well balanced and nutritious.

✓ Should offer variety.

✓ Should be within your family's food budget.

✓ Should fit your time and energy limits.

• When cooking, clean up as you go. Around 50% of cooking time is generally spent waiting. Use that time to wash bowls, utensils, dishes, pots and pans.

• Don't wait for your meals to be done and *then* set the table. Set the table completely with dishes, utensils, condiments and beverages during cooking waiting times. Or better yet, enlist another family member to do so.

• Before making a new recipe, carefully read through the entire recipe. Assemble everything you need first, to ensure you haven't forgotten a needed item. Once you're absolutely sure you have everything necessary, have fun creating your new dish.

• Don't be caught in the kitchen without a kitchen timer. Always set it to sound off a few minutes before the food is supposed to be done. This will avoid burning, plus give you time to make any other last minute preparations. Look for timers that sound a warning beep ten minutes prior and then five minutes prior to the time the actual alarm goes off.

• When your meals are done cooking and you're filling everyone's plate, be sure to organize the food in a complimentary, appetizing way. Put contrasting colors next to each other. Don't overfill the plates. You can always keep extras on the table in case anyone wants a second helping.

• When preparing lots of sandwiches, make them easier to designate which is which. Cut those with mustard horizontally and those with mayonnaise diagonally.

• When cooking a main dish for dinner, double everything so you get two dinners out of it. Refrigerate the second portion for one or two nights later.

• If you, or someone in your family, is on a strict diet, leave a reminder right on the refrigerator door of what can or cannot be eaten. Anyone on a strict diet should keep a journal of what they've eaten so that they can adjust their diet. Plus, they could bring this journal when they visit their doctor to help the physician help them.

- Look for nutritious recipes that you can prepare in one pot, such as chili or stews. Clean-up will be a snap.

- Make two meals at a time; one for tonight and one to freeze.

- If you enjoy a cup of fresh coffee in the morning, it may be well worth it for you to get a coffee maker with a time and brew mechanism. Just fill it with coffee and water, set the timer the evening before and relax with your fresh brew the next day.

- If you love to cook, cookbooks are a godsend. Keep them ready-to-use in the kitchen on a shelf or with bookends on a countertop. However, if you never cook and have little aspiration to do so, donate or dump those old cookbooks.

- Have some frozen veggies left over from last night's dinner? Place them in a plastic bag and freeze them for later use in soups or salads. Why waste money tossing them or wasting time making another trip to the store?

- Save extra trips to the supermarket. Extend the life of food products by refrigerating them, even if they don't require it. This works great for bread, coffee, flour and dried fruits.

- Use your microwave for cooking vegetables, while you're waiting for your main dish to finish cooking.

- If expecting company for dinner, cook everything in the morning or the day before. When your company arrives, warm everything up. You won't be caught running late, or stuck in the kitchen while everyone else is having fun.

- Prepare a whole week's worth of food on Saturdays. Then, you'll just have to heat up your pre-made meals during the week. This is a great idea if you want a healthy meal, but get home too late from work to cook.

- Opt for less time-consuming meals during the week, especially if you work long hours. Pasta, sautéed chicken, or grilled turkey burgers, along with some microwaved veggies are nutritious meals that can be prepared and cooked in record time.

- Have family members start dinner before you get home from work. This is a time-saver, even if it's as simple as preheating the oven, preparing the salad or dicing some vegetables.

- You can't make everybody happy all of the time. So don't even try. If you do, you'll run yourself ragged cooking four different dinners every night. Make it a rule that everybody must eat what you're making for dinner tonight or they can whip up something themselves as a substitute. Be firm here or you'll exhaust yourself.

**Great Idea from . . .**
**Victoria Schellhase**

*I line a cookie sheet with waxed paper and spoon out cookie dough as if for baking, but place it in the freezer instead. Since I'm freezing, not baking the dough, I don't have to worry about it spreading. Therefore, the cookie dough mounds can be very close together.*

*When they are frozen hard, I peel them off and place in a Tupperware container. Since the small dough mounds thaw very quickly, we can have an impromptu treat of homemade cookies quickly and easily, without the additives and preservatives of the commercial brands.*

Victoria Schellhase,
Gaithersburg, MD

Mother of 8 Children
Staff of Life Products
http://www.staffoflife.com

# Monthly Dinner Planner

Make copies of this page and use it as your Monthly Dinner Planner or duplicate a similar form on your computer.

Simply plan your meals for each day of the month. Try to save as much time as possible. For example, if you make a pot of tomato sauce for pasta on Monday, make enough for two meals. You can then either serve pasta again during the same week or freeze the extra sauce for next week.

**Month** _____

**Week Of:**_____
Mon: _____
Tue: _____
Wed: _____
Thu: _____
Fri: _____
Sat: _____
Sun: _____

**Week Of:**_____
Mon: _____
Tue: _____
Wed: _____
Thu: _____
Fri: _____
Sat: _____
Sun: _____

**Week Of:**_____
Mon: _____
Tue: _____
Wed: _____
Thu: _____
Fri: _____
Sat: _____
Sun: _____

**Week Of:**_____
Mon: _____
Tue: _____
Wed: _____
Thu: _____
Fri: _____
Sat: _____
Sun: _____

## Chapter 20

# Recipes

*That is the most fancy, delicious looking chocolate cake I've ever seen! I must clip this recipe!*

**M**any of us are tempted every time we flip through a magazine. As you know, there are certainly no shortage of recipes. However, of all the recipes that are clipped, less than 1% are ever attempted. I've come up with a number of reasons for this strange phenomenon:

✓ There's no specific place to put it, so it gets lost.

✓ We don't set a specific deadline to make it.

✓ We get discouraged by the long list of ingredients.

✓ The effort it's going to take discourages us.

✓ We don't have the necessary ingredients on hand.

✓ We rarely have the extra time it requires to make it.

✓ We get excited about making it as we're clipping, but the excitement wears off quickly.

✓ Another recipe catches our eye; the original one is forgotten.

✓ There's not even a slim chance that we're going to sift through the other 5,000 recipes we have clipped to find this one!

Whatever the reason, those recipes just waiting to be made are clutter! First, get your current recipes under control. Then, organize the *keepers* before you even think about clipping another one.

Gather every recipe you have. If you have some special recipes from a family member or close friend that you'd be very upset to lose, you're going to have to go through your recipes one by one until you find them. However, if all of your recipes are just from newspapers and magazines, I suggest you throw every one of them out.

Pull out your drawer. Walk over to your garbage can and turn the whole thing upside down into it. Yes, dump the entire drawer full. Get a fresh start.

Once you get through the initial shock of doing this, you're all set to start your *organized* recipe collection. By the way, if you really have no aspirations of making new recipes, there's no reason for you to have a recipe collection. Recipes are only worthwhile if you make them.

• Create a "Temporary Recipe System." Get 10 regular, letter-size

> *If you haven't got the time to do it right, when will you find the time to do it over?*
>
> Jeffrey J. Mayer

*Make 4 weekly menus. Start at week one and go through to week four. No one will realize that they're eating meals on an organized system, because it's a four week cycle. They won't get into the "if it's salad, it must be Monday" monotony!*

*Each week has its own shopping list already made out, so when I go to the supermarket I just have to grab the items on the list for that week. Because it's all worked out in advance, I could ensure that it's a healthy and well balanced menu.*

*It's also economical. There is no waste because I only buy exactly what I need for the week.*

*Plus, I could make use of one meal as a foundation for another. For instance, if we have roast chicken, I would buy a chicken too large for one meal and then use leftover chicken in a salad, omelets, paella or risotto. That saves time!*

*Like any system, I'm never strict about it. If I see something on sale at a bargain price, I simply adjust the week's menu accordingly.*

Jackie Jackson
Polar Motor Company
http://www.polarmotor.com

envelopes and label them as follows.

1) Appetizer
2) Bread
3) Chicken
4) Fish
5) Meat
6) Pasta/Rice
7) Salad
8) Soup
9) Vegetable
10) Dessert

• Store all the envelopes in a larger envelope in the kitchen. Whenever you come across a recipe, put it in the appropriate envelope. The only rule is that the maximum number of yet-to-be-attempted recipes, allowed in each folder is 10. The rest must be dumped.

• Get yourself a good recipe box with a set of index cards or recipe cards. This is your "Permanent Recipe Box." Divide it by the categories listed above.

• Once you attempt a recipe, you must decide whether or not you're ever going to make it again. If you are, it should be transferred to your "Permanent Recipe Box." If you're not going to make it again, throw the recipe away.

• If you really have aspirations of attempting a recipe, determine if it is really worth your time and effort. If not, throw it out. If you are going to attempt it, schedule a specific date to do so on your calendar.

• Make a list of all ingredients you need and pick them up on your next trip to the grocery store. The longer the list of ingredients, the less of a chance you're going to actually make it. *(Hint: I rarely clip any recipe with more than 10 ingredients!)*

• If you prefer to store your recipes in a computer database, just make sure the only recipes in there are your permanent recipes.

• The time it takes to prepare a recipe from start to finish could be drastically reduced by using the microwave whenever possible. Check your microwave oven manual for timesaving tips.

• Hold a "New Recipe Party" at your house. Prepare a new recipe with your friends and family. Then you can all enjoy your new dish later on that day.

# Chapter 21

# Laundry

Laundry reminds me of weeds. No matter how many times you clear it out, new laundry always sprouts up instantaneously! It's just one of those chores that is never finished.

A little bit of creative organizing though, goes a long way in helping to significantly reduce the time and effort this endless chore absorbs.

- Place a laundry bag on the back of each bedroom closet door for each family member. Then, tell them it's their responsibility to deliver their full bag to the laundry room when needed. It's a real plus if you can assign each member a turn to chip in with the washing, drying and ironing responsibilities!

- Don't just stand there idle. Put the laundry in the washing machine and do other tasks while it is getting done. Do the same during the dryer cycle.

- Place small laundry baskets, one for each family member, above or near the dryer. Sort clothes, by family member, as you pull them out of the dryer. Have each person pick up their own basket and put their own clothes away.

- If you're not too fond of ironing, wash and dry smaller loads and put them on a hanger right out of the dryer. There won't be as many wrinkles and ironing will be less of a chore.

- If you're making constant trips back and forth to the Laundromat, consider purchasing your own washer and dryer. It will save you mounds of time.

- Sort your whites from your darks prior to wash day. Use old pillowcases—one dark and one light—or a laundry sorter with two to three compartments to separate the clothes you need to wash as you go along. When wash day comes around, everything will be pre-sorted and ready to toss in.

- Aside from undergarments and socks, it's generally unnecessary to wash your pants, sweaters, shirts and dresses every single time you wear them. Unless you spilled something on your clothing, or you were out exercising in them, you can probably get two to three wears before spending the time it takes to wash them.

- Before you put small clothing into the washing machine, get inexpensive mesh bags—usually used for holding hosiery—and

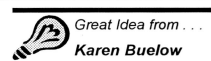

*Great Idea from . . .*
**Karen Buelow**

*When folding laundry, I have a separate basket for each family member, so I avoid going back and forth between rooms and putting clothes away. I also fold all sheets from one bed into its own pillow case.*

Karen Buelow
Germantown, TN

separate each family member's socks, underwear, and other small items into them. When you're done washing, these bags can be tossed into the dryer and dropped in everyone's room later on, without having to sort, re-sort, and then sort again!

- Towels used to dry yourself when you emerge from the shower are still clean. You just washed yourself. Why would the towel be dirty? Hang the towel on a towel rack, so it's dry for the next day. Then, limit your towel washing and drying to once or twice a week.

- Keep a list of items that only get washed occasionally over the washing machine—throw rugs, shower curtains, comforters. When you have less than a full load, just check your list and add one of these items to it. It will also help you to remember to wash those occasional items that are often forgotten.

- Save a trip to the dry cleaner. If at all possible, purchase clothing that doesn't have to be dry cleaned and can be tossed in the washer.

- If you don't have your own washing machine or dryer and use a commercial one, you're probably constantly searching for quarters. Stop at the bank once a week—or go on pay day—and get at least $20 worth of quarters. Keep them in a change purse, specifically to be used for the purpose of washing and drying clothes.

- After doing the wash, immediately iron everything that needs to be. Then, hang these items in your closet. You won't have to waste time each and every morning ironing clothes before work.

- Enlist family members to help with the washing, drying and ironing. Try one of the following:
  - ✓ Have each member do their own wash.
  - ✓ Assign a particular person these duties.
  - ✓ Rotate everyone's schedule so everyone gets a turn.

- Don't wash half-loads. Wait until your laundry bag, hamper or sorter is full. You'll save time, plus money on your energy bill.

- Keep your detergent, bleach and fabric softeners right near your washer and dryer or a nearby storage area. If you do your wash at the laundromat, leave your detergent and other supplies in a plastic container in the car. No sense bringing it back and forth, in and out of the house each week.

- If your budget permits, some laundromats offer an option of washing, drying and folding your clothes for you, to be picked up later. If you don't mind someone else doing your wash, this may be the perfect solution for you.

*Will not man someday make progress in time similar to that he has made in space?*

Pierre Janet

## Chapter 22

# Cleaning and Tidying

Let's face it. Cleaning is not one of life's great joys or pleasures. However, there are a few things that can be done to get the job done quicker so that we don't waste the entire day and we don't exhaust ourselves. An organized cleaning system and a little motivation will help eliminate clutter, accumulated dirt and dust, food particles, crumbs and other unsightly stuff that can affect our health and the life of our home furnishings.

- Don't do it all yourself. Assign specific cleaning tasks to each family member. If you like, you can even rotate the responsibilies so everyone has a turn at each task.

- Don't make 50 trips up and down the stairs. When you have an item that has to go upstairs, leave it near the step. When you have to go upstairs later, gather and bring everything up in one trip.

- Keep a laundry basket both at the top and bottom of the stairs. Items going down go in the upstairs basket; items going up go in the downstairs basket. Switch baskets as you go up and downstairs.

- Use a caddy with a handle to carry around your cleansers, furniture polish and cleaning rags so you don't have to keep returning to your cleaning storage area.

- Play upbeat music while you clean and organize. It will make you feel energetic.

- Do one chore a day, either before work or after work. This way you can enjoy the weekend, instead of spending it doing housework.

- There are a plethora of cleaning products. However, there's no reason to waste your time, money and energy, buying and using a million different ones to clean your home. Minimize. Buy one all-purpose cleaner for all your cleaning needs.

- If you have a number of small wastepaper baskets around your home, don't empty each one outside individually. Carry a large, plastic garbage bag to each wastepaper basket, starting from the furthest one and working your way through the house. Then dump the large bag outside once.

**Great Idea from . . .**
**Julie Knecht**

*If your home has carpeting, you obviously want it to look like new for a long time. After all, carpeting is expensive.*

*Keep a terrycloth hand towel easily accessible.*

*If a soda is accidentally spilled on it, immediately grab the hand towel, place it on the spill and step on it. Most of the soda will be soaked up on the towel instead of the carpet.*

*Of course, you'll have to complete the cleanup job with some foam rug cleaner afterwards, but initializing cleanup with the towel first, eliminates the stain from setting in.*

Julie Knecht, Ormond Beach, FL

Julie is my aunt and godmother. She has two sons (Michael Sr. & Bobby), a daughter-in-law (Barbara) and two grandchildren (Lauren and Michael Jr.)

*If I had to live my
life over again,
I would have
waxed less
and listened more.*

Erma Bombeck

- If you can afford it, it is well worth the money to hire a house-keeper on a regular basis. Hire a cleaning team once a year before the big holiday gathering to clean your house from top to bottom.

- Immediately separate your recyclable items—paper, plastic and cans—from your regular garbage by having separate, colored and labeled garbage cans. If the cans are different colors, they'll be easily identifiable to all family members.

- Buy pots and pans with Teflon coating. It will save you quite a bit of clean-up time.

- Have your family take their shoes off as soon as they walk into the house. You won't have to clean the rug as often.

- Keep some folded, empty trash liners at the bottom of each garbage can. When you throw away the garbage, you'll have a new one immediately, without having to make an extra trip to get one.

- Don't leave dirty dishes in the dishwasher overnight. Run the dishwasher cycle in the evening while watching television or tidying up, so that everything is clean and ready to use in the morning.

- Tired of scrubbing the shower? What a waste of time! There's a product available in most supermarkets called "Clean Shower™." After you take a shower, just spray it on the shower tiles and curtain and walk away. No scrubbing needed!

- Empty your garbage cans and recyclable containers as soon as they start getting full, otherwise you're going to spend time picking up the overflow of trash.

- Keep a "Pet Hair Pick-up Roller" handy if you have a cat or dog. These sticky rollers can be rolled over the surface of your furniture, drapery and clothing to quickly remove hair and lint.

- Don't forget about the outside of your home. Put outdoor cleaning tasks such as window washing and sweeping on your cleaning schedule so you remember to keep it up.

- Cleaning done on a well-organized schedule, systematically, will get the job done quickly and keep your place looking great. Plus, it will help prolong the life of your possessions.

- Set your own rules. There's no law that says you have to clean every single week. You decide how often it needs to get done. Then, come up with a written schedule for doing so.

- Consider each cleaning task you do a great accomplishment. Reward yourself for doing so. It will motivate you to help keep everything tidy and organized.

## Chapter 23

❖ ❖ ❖ ❖ ❖ ❖ ❖ ❖ ❖ ❖ ❖ ❖ ❖ ❖ ❖ ❖ ❖

# Decorating, Remodeling
# and Repair

I enjoy watching the Home and Garden Channel on television. It carries programming that is just loaded with great tips and ideas for decorating, remodeling, refurbishing, installation, quick fix-it jobs and garden ideas. Of course, I don't spend every minute in my own home tackling each of these projects. However, every idea certainly gets me thinking more creatively when it comes to effective organization.

- If you purchase "Assembly Required" products, you probably have random packages of extra nuts, washers and screws that manufacturers include. If you have no idea what these items go with, dump them. And remember, next time you purchase a *put it together yourself* product, immediately label the little plastic bag of widgets.

- If you own a lot of collectibles—baseball cards, figurines, spoons, dolls—use available information sources such as magazines or appropriate web sites to get ideas on how to arrange them in an organized manner. Purchase the manufacturers suggested organizing containers to prolong the life of your collections.

- Before rearranging or redecorating your home, plan ahead. Sketch your thoughts out on paper. Carefully measure, especially prior to buying expensive furniture.

- When remodeling, take before-and-after photos. You'll be able to preserve the memory, plus you'll have proof of improvement value for tax related purposes.

- Before moving around heavy furniture, just to discover you don't like the way it looks, consider first using one of the many software products available. They can help you plan your design to ensure you're going to like the way it looks, *before* you move the furniture.

- Enlist some friends to help you paint your house. To entice them, throw a painting party. You supply the pizza, sandwiches, soda . . . and maybe some chocolate chip cookies for an additional incentive!

- Have you ever put aside items that were broken with the expectation that you'll get them fixed one day? Chances are, these items are still where you left them and they're still broken. When this situation occurs, determine if the item is really worth the repair or not. If it isn't, throw it away. If it is, immediately schedule a date and time

*Time is the great art of man.*

Napoleon

on your calendar to take care of the necessary repair—and get it repaired when the date rolls around.

- Prior to hanging artwork, take the time to sketch out your thoughts on paper, especially if you're planning on hanging a number of items in a creative arrangement. Measure carefully before hanging. Use a level to ensure pictures are straight. Draw a pencil mark where the top of the frame will be and stand back to ensure it meets your requirements, *before* you start hammering.

- Disorganized, tangled wires are not only unattractive, but are hazardous. Disconnect any wires that are not being used. Ensure that no one will trip over wires; run them along baseboards and behind furniture.

- Organize wires from electronics and appliances into one tube. "Split-loom Tubing" or "Wire Covers" can be purchased in houseware, hardware or electronics stores.

- When redecorating, keep color schemes simple and light to make space appear larger.

- If you loan a tool to someone, immediately set a date on your calendar when you expect it back. If it hasn't been returned to you by then, contact the borrower and ask how much longer she/he will need it. Then, write the new expecting date on your calendar again. Follow up until you receive your tool back.

- If you're building something with someone who brought his/her own set of tools over, be very careful not to get those tools mixed up with yours. Code your tools with labels or a spot of florescent paint for quick identification.

- When purchasing furniture, look for both form and function. For instance, consider a coffee table with a built-in cabinet for storage, a lamp with an attached magazine rack or a bench with storage space under the seat.

- When you purchase Do-it-Yourself furniture and appliances, don't attempt to put it together without first reading the directions. I know how intimidating and long some of those direction booklets are. However, it is frustrating and a waste of time to skip reading the instructions, put it together and then discover you missed a very important step that you wouldn't have missed had you been following the correct procedures. Now you have to start over again.

- Minimize furniture and knick-knacks. Are you saying, "It will look so bare?" Would you say that about a sunset, the ocean or the sky? Empty space is peaceful to look at. It allows you to free your mind and release your creative juices. There's also less work, since there is less to clean, less to buy and less to break. Think about it.

*Our life is frittered away by detail. Simplify. Simplify.*

Henry David Thoreau

## Chapter 24

# Health, Nutrition and Grooming

Billy Crystal used to say, "It's better to look marvelous than to feel marvelous." That statement always got a chuckle, but in reality, I say "It's better to look marvelous *AND* feel marvelous."

Time management and productivity are directly related to your health and your positive outlook on life. The better you feel internally, the more productive you're going to be! The more you dress for success, the more productive you will be! Don't settle for one or the other. Always strive for both.

- Before calling or visiting your physician or dentist, jot down your symptoms and questions. You'll remember to ask all questions pertaining to your health and medications. Schedule regular medical check-ups. Good health is equal to higher productivity.

- If someone in your family has high/low blood pressure, purchase a blood pressure monitor. Keep a journal indicating the systolic and diastolic pressures, time of day and any other necessary circumstances. This will help your doctor to help you or your family members achieve optimum health.

- The next time you have to write a membership payment out to the gym you go to, decide if you really want to spend the money or the time it takes you to get back and forth. If you make exercise part of your daily routine, you can discipline yourself to eat moderately and exercise at home, or walk to work. It will save you more time than you can imagine.

- Try your very best to avoid heavy meals. They drain your energy, thus executing poor use of your time.

- Don't skip meals. Take the time to refuel with low-fat, high-energy choices.

- Stretch before and after you exercise. Skipping stretching will not save time. In fact, you're liable to spend time at the doctor's office or home in bed after pulling a muscle.

- Rather than exercising in the middle of the day, exercise first thing in the morning. This way you only have to shower once.

- Get a good night's sleep—at least 7 hours or more. Adequate rest will help you to be alert, on schedule and effective tomorrow.

*Great Idea from . . .*
*Margie Pisano*

*Always keep an Emery board in your purse. You'll be prepared for a quick-fix if you break a nail.*

*In addition, carry clear nail polish with you when wearing panty hose. If you get a run, simply put some polish at the top and bottom of the run to prevent it from getting any worse.*

*A little bit of planning is worth a pound of prevention.*

Margie Pisano, Jersey City, NJ

Margie, my mom, is married to my dad, Mike. They have one other daughter; my sister, Jude. They also have a dog named Heidi and a cat named Luke.

- Get an attractive, easy-to-maintain haircut. It will eliminate constant trips back and forth to the hairdresser, plus you won't waste hours drying and styling every morning.

- Exercise a little bit each day; a full aerobic workout or a walk around the block. It will dramatically increase your energy and productivity.

- Looking for some time to exercise. Instead of taking your car to the car wash, wash it yourself. You'll be burning off those calories in no time!

- Motivate yourself to exercise by doing so with a friend. Agree on a time of day that would be good for both of you. It's the perfect time to catch up and you'll be staying fit at the same time.

- Can't find time to exercise? Go to bed 20 minutes earlier, so that you can wake up 20 minutes earlier.

- Take a walk with your spouse. Catch up on your day. Talk about your dreams. Do these together and you'll be exercising and communicating at the same time.

- Remember, 20 minutes of exercise a day is nothing compared to the 1,440 minutes a day we all have.

- Organize pills into pillboxes with compartments for days of the week. This way, you won't forget to take them when you need to.

- Schedule time to exercise on your calendar. Keep that date, just as you would any other.

- Keep a journal of what you eat every day. Note your energy levels. Stay away from those foods that drag your energy level down.

- Take time to laugh each and every day. Ever hear "laughter is the best medicine"? A little bit of laughter each day relieves your anxiety, reduces your stress level and increases your productivity.

- Always look your very best, whether you're going to an important meeting or if you're working at home. Doing so will inspire you to push ahead and succeed.

- Eat with good nutrition in mind—more fruits and vegetables, less fat, salt and sugar. By the way, sugar really drags some people down. If you're affected by sugar, your productivity may drop after a few days of candy bars, cookies and soda. Avoid it if it affects you this way.

- Be careful of smoking and excessive drinking. They do nothing to benefit your health or your productivity. In fact they greatly increase health risks which create obstacles to your accomplishments.

- Keep good medical records for each family member. Include medical histories, immunizations, blood pressure and cholesterol readings, known allergies, test results and current/past medications.

*It is better to be prepared for an opportunity and not have one than to have an opportunity and not be prepared.*

Whitney Young, Jr.

# Chapter 25

# Photographs

Photographs are wonderful for bringing back sweet memories and initiating a funny conversation. They're proof of exotic destinations we've traveled to and mementos of special times.

If you treasure your photographs, it's essential to organize and protect them. Doing so will help ensure that they don't get ripped, curled, crumpled or lost. Future generations can then enjoy them for years to come.

- Be prepared. Keep your camera loaded and always keep extra film on hand. You never know when the opportunity for the perfect family photograph will arise.

- Make it a point to schedule a date and time to bring any undeveloped film lying around to your photo developer. Don't allow yourself to take one more photograph until you do so.

- Designate a "Film Drop-off Box." This is where family members can leave film to be developed. Assign someone in your family a specific date and time to deliver and pick-up.

- When your photos have been developed, jot down who, what, where and when on the back of the photos. Then, organize them in an album or scrapbook. If you can't do it immediately, schedule a date and time on your calendar.

- Save a trip to the photo developer by mailing in your film. You'll receive your photos back within a few days, via the mail or the Internet. Give Mystic Photo Labs a try. Their service is excellent and their prices are very reasonable.
  http://www.mysticcolorlab.com

- If you already have 99 shoeboxes filled with photos that are in no particular order, separate photos by year or event and store them in labeled photo albums or photo boxes. This may take a few days, depending on your backlog. You may want to ask a friend or relative to help you sort them. Send doubles to people in the photo, even if you haven't heard from them in years. It's a terrific way to get back in touch with each other.

- Get a digital camera. Once you take a picture, you can show it to whoever you want to via the Internet without spending a dime in postage or the time it takes to send them through the U.S. Mail. Send it to them in an attached file or post it on a website.

 *Great Idea from . . .*
**Karen Buelow**

*I always travel with a disposable camera in my car in case of an accident. This way at the scene, I will have proof of any damage or other circumstances.*

*I also keep spare, disposable cameras in a diaper bag for spontaneous shots of my children. Once, at a big church event, the historian's camera failed to work, so I had a spare to lend her!*

Karen Buelow, Germantown, TN

# Chapter 26

❖ ❖ ❖ ❖ ❖ ❖ ❖ ❖ ❖ ❖ ❖ ❖ ❖ ❖ ❖ ❖ ❖

# Rummage Sales

W ant to declutter, plus make a little extra pocket change? You can do so without actually throwing anything out. A yard sale or rummage sale may be the perfect answer!

Where I live in Wisconsin, rummage sales are plentiful during the summer months. People really seem to love them. I guess everyone enjoys a bargain.

Although I would certainly not recommend that you spend a lot of time at yard sales if you're a Pack Rat, I certainly am all for you *hosting* one.

• Tell everyone you know about the sale. Run an ad in your local newspaper. Put up posters and signs at nearby intersections if your town allows.

• Be very specific about the date and time of your sale. If you don't tell people the sale is on Saturday, June 4, from 10:00AM to 4:00PM, people will show up on your doorstep at 7:30 in the morning, or 9:00 at night!

• Involve the kids. Let them reap some of the benefits.

• Make the atmosphere of your sale as inviting as possible. Cover tables with decorative tablecloths. Play soft music in the background. Dress nicely. Instill an air of friendliness. Have free refreshments like lemonade and cookies.

• Organize items into categories such as clothing, games, dinnerware, collectibles, blankets, and so on.

• Mark all prices clearly. Make sure they're reasonable. In fact, make sure they're a bargain. Use "Buy One - Get One Free" tactics. Offer items at a volume discount.

• Make sure you have bags and/or boxes for customers to place their purchases in.

• Accept cash only. Have plenty of change on hand. Never leave the money unattended. Use a calculator.

• Don't price items with odd amounts like $2.49 or $7.22. Price in increments of $0.25, such as $5.50 or $11.75 or $4.00.

• If you don't sell it, you'll be dumping it. Towards the end of the day, drastically reduce your prices.

### Great Idea from . . .
### Kathy Pankow

*I like to host rummage sales. To save time, I keep ready-to-use price stickers on hand. Whenever I have something that I want to put in the next sale, I think up a fair price and immediately place a price sticker on it. Then I place the item in the designated rummage sale boxes, which we keep in the basement.*

*When I'm ready to have a rummage sale, everything is in one area and ready to be sold. I don't have to go all over the house trying to remember what I wanted to put up for sale. Since I priced everything out ahead, there's another detail I don't have to worry about.*

Kathy Pankow, Hubertus, WI

Kathy, a magazine merchandiser, is married to Paul, a systems technician for Ameritech. They have three children: Craig, Alissa and Ross.

## Chapter 27

# Moving

**M**any people absolutely hate the thought of moving. After all, packing and unpacking heavy furniture and bulky boxes is certainly not a picnic in the park!

Yet, it really doesn't have to be such a daunting task. To assure a successful move with little or no stress, the secret is to plan it carefully and to use systems that will ensure a smooth transition.

- Don't move everything you own. The rule is . . . if you don't use it now, don't bother to move it. You won't use it later.

- Don't leave your packing until the last minute. Begin early and you'll be prepared well-ahead of time when moving day arrives.

- Create a "Moving Checklist" to ensure you do everything you have to do to make this a stress-free, successful move. Don't leave all of the tasks ahead to memory alone.

- When you are moving, don't mark every box *Stuff*. Pack related items together. Clearly and specifically label each box.

- Color-code boxes with self-stick yellow dots for those the movers should move to your kitchen, red dots for those boxes to go to the bedroom and so on. Go to your new house ahead of time and place a corresponding colored dot on the appropriate rooms. You won't have to unpack everything to determine where it goes.

- If you don't want the expense of having to purchase boxes for your move, ask one of your local stores if they can spare any. Many usually give them up happily and for free!

- Before moving old furniture into your new home, measure the dimensions. Be sure it fits through doorways and up stairs, before you have it moved there. The same goes for window treatments.

- Write out directions to your new home, coming from north, south, east and west. Leave these instructions right by your telephone to give to anyone visiting. In addition, keep a small local map near the directions, just in case.

- Enlist family and friends to help you move. To entice them, throw a moving party. You supply the food and beverages.

- If you move every few years, decorate with neutral colors. This way, you won't have to buy new things every time you move.

*Those who rush, arrive first at the grave.*

Spanish Proverb

# Moving Checklist

Make copies of this page and use it as your Moving Checklist or duplicate a similar form on your computer.

Simply add in any details not already listed. Then, determine the appropriate start date and due dates on your calendar and schedule appropriately. Check off each task as you complete it. Happy moving!

## 4-6 Weeks

___ Begin calling for moving company estimates and make a decision on which company you're going to use.
___ Make a list of places to forward your change of address to as you go through your mail.
___ Have your W-2's forwarded.
___ Notify schools.
___ Get medical and dental records.
___ Check out churches in the new community.
___ Get boxes from the grocery store or other places.
___ Start to use up your food.
___ Return anything you have borrowed.
___ Put out a box for "moving items" like the mover telephone number, the measuring tape, packing materials, keys to the new place and important papers.
___ Pack up your out-of-season clothes.
___ Clean your curtains and blankets.
___ Pack up your attic and/or basement.
___ Make a survival kit for the first night (flashlight, batteries, hammer, screwdriver, paper plates, can opener, snacks, cleaning supplies, garbage bags, scissors, first aid kit, tape, toilet paper, linens, towels and anything else you may need.)
___ Order new address labels and checks.
___ Pack up books.
___ _____
___ _____

## 2-3 Weeks

___ Go through possessions and donate things you no longer want to charity.
___ Notify the utility companies of your new place and when you need everything turned on.
___ Pack pictures and mirrors.
___ Pack up audio cassettes, CD-roms and video tapes.
___ Tune up your cars.
___ Discontinue paper delivery.
___ Call your insurance agent for any changes.
___ Give children a box for their special things.
___ Arrange to have your utilities turned off.
___ _____
___ _____

## 1 Week

___ Fill out forms at the post office to forward mail.
___ Send change of address cards with your new address and phone number to friends and family.
___ Get a babysitter to watch kids as you move.

___ Decide where you want to put everything.
___ Keep packing things in labeled boxes.
___ Pick up any dry cleaning.
___ _____
___ _____

## 2 Days

___ Tape up bottles like cleaners and shampoo, so they don't leak.
___ Get rid of any flammables.
___ Pack up curtains and blinds.
___ If possible, spray your new house with bug spray.
___ Clean stove.
___ _____
___ _____

## The Day Before

___ Defrost freezer.
___ Pack personal things.
___ _____
___ _____

## Moving Day

___ Ensure bedding is labeled to be unloaded first.
___ Tape loose screws under the furniture they go to.
___ Vacuum and do a final inspection.
___ Lock windows and doors.
___ _____
___ _____

## After Your Arrival

___ Take the family on a walk of the new neighborhood.
___ Enroll children in school.
___ Visit stores.
___ Inquire about public transportation.
___ Change address on driver's license.
___ Place local emergency numbers by the telephone.
___ Get babysitter references.
___ Get a phone book.
___ Get information from the Chamber of Commerce about your new city.
___ Write out directions to your home so you are prepared when anyone asks how to get to your new home.
___ _____
___ _____

## Chapter 28

# Parties

Parties are meant to be so much fun. Why is it then, that often they're the source of such stress? While this anxiety is sometimes due to unexpected guests showing up or some other reason out of your control, oftentimes it's due to lack of sufficient planning.

The good parties—you know, those that have the near-perfect mix of fun, entertainment and food—are *planned parties.*

- Before guests arrive, organize where each guest will sit by putting place cards on the table. If you're serving, make sure your chair is the one closest to the kitchen.

- Plan your party meals carefully; at least a week or more before the party. Don't forget to ask your guests about diet restrictions or make sure you have a variety of foods to choose from.

- Don't leave all those details to memory alone. Create a "Party Checklist" and ensure everything is taken care of.

- Make a list of all groceries you have to pick up. Prepare meals in advance. Assign tasks to members of your family for the big day.

- Planning food for a crowd? To avoid wasted time and a refrigerator full of leftovers, use this guide. Just multiply the individual serving size by the number of guests—or servings—you anticipate:

  Appetizers .......................... 5 pieces (1/2 cup)
  Meat/Poultry/Fish .............. 4 ounces
  Side Dishes ....................... 1/2 cup
  Condiments ....................... 2 teaspoons (mustard, mayo, etc.)
  Dips ................................. 1 tablespoon
  Ice Cream .......................... 1/2 cup

- Take plates, bowls, glasses, utensils and coffee cups out in advance. You'll be sure to have everything you need within arms reach, without having to fumble while your guests are waiting.

- When having a dinner party, instead of making several trips from the kitchen, use a tray. If you have lots of food to carry in and you hold parties often, consider using a rolling cart.

- If you're planning to have your party outside, come up with a plan in case of rain. Can it be moved inside or can you set a rain date?

*We don't want to miss anything in our times; perhaps there are finer times, but the present one is ours.*

Jean-Paul Sartre

- If you're just having a casual party—such as a Super Bowl get-together or children's birthday party—consider using paper plates and cups. Clean up will be a breeze.

- Keep a journal of the parties you host. This is great for future reference, such as using it to avoid serving or wearing the same thing next time you entertain the same guests. Some items to include:

  ✓ meal/dessert you served
  ✓ type of party (formal, casual, theme, etc.)
  ✓ what you/other family members wore
  ✓ names of your guests
  ✓ what your guests brought
  ✓ special diet restrictions
  ✓ party favors

- You don't have to take the time to make everything from scratch. Have your party catered or have everyone bring their own dish.

- Prepare your meals ahead of time. If you make everything the day before, it will just have to be heated up the next day when your guests arrive. The host or hostess shouldn't have to be stuck in the kitchen, while guests are present and having fun.

- Instead of holding an indoor party, consider an outdoor barbecue. There's less to clean up later and less to prepare beforehand.

- If you're holding an adults-only party, get a babysitter to watch your children for a few hours. This way, you won't have to tend to your guests and your kids at the same time.

- When holding a children's party, come up with a planned schedule of events so the kids don't get bored. Consider various games, a dancing contest, time to eat, time to open presents, story time, etc. Make an agenda and review it with everyone at the beginning of the party. Everyone will know what to expect and look forward to.

- If you have a party where the guests don't know each other, consider nametags and ice-breaker games. Everyone will feel more comfortable and have a better time.

- Don't cry over spilled milk. In case something doesn't work out exactly as expected, simply make due. If you burnt the roast, order out for pizza. If the dog ate the beautiful cake you just baked, pick up a store bought one. Bring the party inside if it rains. You get the picture. Don't get annoyed at something you can't change. Make the best of every situation.

- Assign after-party clean-up duties to a group of people. Clean-up will be quicker and you won't get exhausted doing it all yourself.

---

*Carpe Diem!*

*(Seize the Day!)*

Horace

# Party Checklist

Make copies of this page and use it as your Party Checklist or duplicate a similar form on your computer.

Simply add in any details not already listed. Then, determine the appropriate start date and due dates on your calendar and schedule appropriately. Check off each task as you complete it.

## 3 Weeks Ahead

___ Decide on a party theme.
___ Decide where the party will be held.
___ Make any necessary reservations and pay any deposits.
___ Create the guest list.
___ Purchase invitations.
___ Send out or call with invitations (Be sure to include the Theme, the Date of the Party, Start Time, End Time, Place and any other necessary specifications.)
___ Select and purchase decorations.
___ Select and hire the catering service or other help if needed.
___ Reserve any necessary party costumes.

## 2 Weeks Ahead

___ Plan the menu.
___ Write a meal preparation schedule, noting what needs to be done in advance, and what needs to be prepared the day of the event. Prioritize this list.
___ Make notes of special equipment, additional seating or serving pieces you may need.
___ Buy any paper goods.
___ Buy soda, wine, juice and other beverages.
___ Make place cards for your guests.
___ Purchase party favors.
___ Decide on appropriate music and pick up any necessary equipment.

## 1 Week Ahead

___ Clean and press tablecloths and cloth napkins.
___ Decide what you'll wear. Try it on to make sure it fits. Adjust accordingly.
___ Gather chairs or tables that you're borrowing.
___ Call any guests who haven't responded.
___ Schedule appropriate party games. If this is a children's party, create a schedule. Reserve any necessary equipment.
___ Order the cake and arrange to have it picked up or delivered the day before the party.
___ If you're having a barbecue, ensure you have enough gas for the grill.

## 1 - 3 Days Ahead

___ Make your shopping list. Be sure to check your refrigerator and/or pantry.
___ Go grocery shopping.
___ Clean the house.
___ Polish serving dishes, utensils and so on.
___ Prepare make-ahead recipes and refrigerate or freeze them.
___ Pick up any party costumes.
___ Have a first-aid kit together, just in case.

## 1 Day Ahead

___ Set up the beverage area.
___ Select music.
___ Arrange decorations.
___ Take out serving pieces.
___ Set the table.
___ Put place cards at the appropriate settings.
___ Thaw any frozen party foods.
___ Coordinate any last minute arrangements.

## Day of Party

___ Make the remaining recipes.
___ Buy ice, flowers and anything else perishable.
___ Take a final check.
___ Allow 2 hours before guests arrive to catch your breath and take care of yourself.
___ Get dressed.
___ Await arrival.
___ Have a blast!

Party Theme_____

Guest of Honor_____

Date_____

Start Time_____

End Time_____

Place_____

> *We do not remember days, we remember moments.*
>
> Cesare Pavese

## Chapter 29

# Holidays

Tangled strings of colorful lights. Last minute gift worries. Pine needles covering the floor. Presents to wrap. Cards to send. The big day is almost here and you haven't even gotten started yet!

'Tis the season to get organized!

The holidays are meant to be enjoyed. It should be a fun, stress-free experience for you and your loved ones. Don't let disorganization trap you into holiday chaos.

- When out-of-town guests are visiting, organize a nice "Welcome Basket" for them. Include toiletries, extra wrapped toothbrushes, maps and a guidebook. Be creative. They'll appreciate your kindness and won't have to waste time that could be spent with you and your family, running out to a store for forgotten or needed items.

- Don't do your holiday shopping at the height of the season. The lines will be too long. There's a good chance the item you want will be sold out. You'll waste a lot of time and exhaust yourself from the stress. Go shopping a month or two early and enjoy the holiday shopping experience.

- Before you do your holiday shopping, make a list with appropriate names and some gift ideas. Look through your newspaper circulars for possibilities before going to the store. Jot down your budget for each person. Indicate any appropriate sizes. Doing these things will save you time, money and aggravation.

- If you decorate for the holidays, keep your holiday decorations organized and clean in covered, plastic, see-through storage boxes. You'll probably need one for your Christmas or Hanukkah decorations and another for all the other holidays that come up the rest of the year. Store your Christmas/Hanukkah box in a storage room, attic or basement since you only need it once a year. Your other box however, since you'll probably be in it from time to time— should be in a more accessible area—maybe on the shelf over your coat closet or under your bed.

- Make sure your holiday lights are working *before* you put them on your tree and windows. While you're at it, ensure you have any necessary extension cords and light timers.

- Rather than holding it in your house, why not rent a hall for your holiday bash? Have it catered. Enlist family members and friends to help with arrangements. The burden won't be on you alone.

- Plan out your gift budget on paper. Include names and budget amounts. Decide on gifts based on those amounts. Doing this before you go to the store will save time and money.

- If you have a large, holiday family gift list and shopping is going to take quite a bit of time and money, why not get together with your family members and draw one name each out of a basket? This way everyone only has to buy one gift. Limit the amount that can be spent. (Here's another idea: before family members put their names in the basket, have them include choices of three gifts they may like. This will make it easier for the gift givers, and will ensure the recipients get something they will like and use.

- Wrap holiday gifts well ahead of time. If you wrap gifts as soon as you buy them and stick a discreet label on each one to identify the recipient, you won't be caught running late at the last minute.

- Order holiday cards the first week of October from a mail order company such as Current (http://www.currentcatalog.com). Address and write them out a little at a time from Halloween through Thanksgiving. A computer database and printed labels could make this job a snap! Mail them the day after Thanksgiving.

- Create a permanent record of holiday cards sent and received. You won't be caught wondering whether or not you sent or received a card a year ago.

- Consider sending holiday postcards instead of holiday greeting cards. They require less postage and take less time to write out.

- Don't stand in the post office waiting to purchase stamps during the busy holiday season. You'll be in there all day! Order holiday stamps through the mail or buy them at the post office well ahead of time.

- Donate old Christmas cards to the St. Jude's Ranch for Children. The children cut up your old cards, make new ones and then sell them to finance their facility. (St. Jude's Ranch for Children, Box 985, 100 Saint Jude's Street, Boulder City, NV 89005)

- If you hang holiday lights on your tree, don't take them off and put them away in a tangled mess. Wrap them around the original box they came in or around a 12"x12" piece of cardboard. Cut a small slit in the end of the cardboard to slip the plug end into.

- Turn the "undecorating" into a party. Get together with your family and/or invite friends over. Serve refreshments. Play music. The chore will be finished quicker and everyone will have a great time.

*Time is a sort of river of passing events, and strong is its current!*

Marcus Aurelius Antoninus

# Holiday Card Log

Make copies of this page and use it as your Holiday Card Log or duplicate a similar form on your computer.

Simply fill in names, addresses and any other appropriate information. Write in the current year in the spaces provided. Then check off each person that you send a card to and each one that you receive a card from.

Year  Sent  Rcv'd

____  ____  ____    Name_____
____  ____  ____    Address_____
____  ____  ____    City_____ ST_____ ZIP _____
____  ____  ____    Phone_____
____  ____  ____    Children's Names or Other Notes_____

Year  Sent  Rcv'd

____  ____  ____    Name_____
____  ____  ____    Address_____
____  ____  ____    City_____ ST_____ ZIP _____
____  ____  ____    Phone_____
____  ____  ____    Children's Names or Other Notes_____

Year  Sent  Rcv'd

____  ____  ____    Name_____
____  ____  ____    Address_____
____  ____  ____    City_____ ST_____ ZIP _____
____  ____  ____    Phone_____
____  ____  ____    Children's Names or Other Notes_____

Year  Sent  Rcv'd

____  ____  ____    Name_____
____  ____  ____    Address_____
____  ____  ____    City_____ ST_____ ZIP _____
____  ____  ____    Phone_____
____  ____  ____    Children's Names or Other Notes_____

Year  Sent  Rcv'd

____  ____  ____    Name_____
____  ____  ____    Address_____
____  ____  ____    City_____ ST_____ ZIP _____
____  ____  ____    Phone_____
____  ____  ____    Children's Names or Other Notes_____

Year  Sent  Rcv'd

____  ____  ____    Name_____
____  ____  ____    Address_____
____  ____  ____    City_____ ST_____ ZIP _____
____  ____  ____    Phone_____
____  ____  ____    Children's Names or Other Notes_____

# Birthdays and Special Occasions

Make copies of this page and use it to track birthdays/special occasions or duplicate a similar form on your computer.

Simply add appropriate name(s) under each appropriate month. Indicate the day of the month and the event code. Create your own event codes for those not listed.

| B=Birthday | A=Anniversary | H=Holiday | G=Graduation |
| --- | --- | --- | --- |
| __ = _____ | __ = _____ | __ = _____ | __ = _____ |

### January

| Day | Event | Name |
| --- | --- | --- |
| ___ | ___ | _____ |
| ___ | ___ | _____ |
| ___ | ___ | _____ |
| ___ | ___ | _____ |
| ___ | ___ | _____ |
| ___ | ___ | _____ |

### February

| Day | Event | Name |
| --- | --- | --- |
| ___ | ___ | _____ |
| ___ | ___ | _____ |
| ___ | ___ | _____ |
| ___ | ___ | _____ |
| ___ | ___ | _____ |
| ___ | ___ | _____ |

### March

| Day | Event | Name |
| --- | --- | --- |
| ___ | ___ | _____ |
| ___ | ___ | _____ |
| ___ | ___ | _____ |
| ___ | ___ | _____ |
| ___ | ___ | _____ |
| ___ | ___ | _____ |

### April

| Day | Event | Name |
| --- | --- | --- |
| ___ | ___ | _____ |
| ___ | ___ | _____ |
| ___ | ___ | _____ |
| ___ | ___ | _____ |
| ___ | ___ | _____ |

### May

| Day | Event | Name |
| --- | --- | --- |
| ___ | ___ | _____ |
| ___ | ___ | _____ |
| ___ | ___ | _____ |
| ___ | ___ | _____ |
| ___ | ___ | _____ |

### June

| Day | Event | Name |
| --- | --- | --- |
| ___ | ___ | _____ |
| ___ | ___ | _____ |
| ___ | ___ | _____ |
| ___ | ___ | _____ |
| ___ | ___ | _____ |

### July

| Day | Event | Name |
| --- | --- | --- |
| ___ | ___ | _____ |
| ___ | ___ | _____ |
| ___ | ___ | _____ |
| ___ | ___ | _____ |
| ___ | ___ | _____ |

### August

| Day | Event | Name |
| --- | --- | --- |
| ___ | ___ | _____ |
| ___ | ___ | _____ |
| ___ | ___ | _____ |
| ___ | ___ | _____ |
| ___ | ___ | _____ |

### September

| Day | Event | Name |
| --- | --- | --- |
| ___ | ___ | _____ |
| ___ | ___ | _____ |
| ___ | ___ | _____ |
| ___ | ___ | _____ |
| ___ | ___ | _____ |

### October

| Day | Event | Name |
| --- | --- | --- |
| ___ | ___ | _____ |
| ___ | ___ | _____ |
| ___ | ___ | _____ |
| ___ | ___ | _____ |
| ___ | ___ | _____ |

### November

| Day | Event | Name |
| --- | --- | --- |
| ___ | ___ | _____ |
| ___ | ___ | _____ |
| ___ | ___ | _____ |
| ___ | ___ | _____ |
| ___ | ___ | _____ |

### December

| Day | Event | Name |
| --- | --- | --- |
| ___ | ___ | _____ |
| ___ | ___ | _____ |
| ___ | ___ | _____ |
| ___ | ___ | _____ |
| ___ | ___ | _____ |

**Chapter 30**

# Gifts

Whenever I buy a gift for someone, I really try my best to get something that person will use and enjoy. After all, if they don't, then it is nothing but clutter and I never want to contribute to someone else's clutter!

- When I'm not sure what to buy, I just ask the other person if there's something special they may like. Although some people may be really opposed to this idea because it won't be a surprise, it really ensures that I never waste time, money or energy buying something that is just going to be tossed in a dark closet forever.

- If you don't want to ask the actual recipient for his or her choice of a gift, ask their family members or friends. They may be able to give you the perfect idea.

- Ask for gifts, and give gifts, that don't clutter. There are lots of great choices including dinner gift certificates, theatre tickets, music lessons, a day at the spa or a vacation!

- Rather than trying to find the perfect gift at the last minute, when you see something in a store that you know someone would just love, pick it up now and store it until his or her birthday or for another appropriate occasion.

- Keep a written log of people you frequently purchase gifts for. Include their name, clothing sizes, hobbies and any other information that will make it easier for you to buy a gift for that person when a special occasion rolls around.

- When you think of a great gift idea, but you don't have time to buy it immediately, jot the idea down in your gift log. You'll make sure you don't forget what your idea was when you're ready to buy it.

- Consider a greeting card organizer to organize cards for birthdays, anniversaries, holidays and other events. These look like a notebook, except that each page has a pocket to hold cards for a specific month. There is usually space for you to pencil in events for that month. Since you can easily see what's coming up, you'll never send out a greeting card late. Plus, you can buy cards ahead of time and store them in your organizer until the date rolls around.

- If you're planning to have a gift wrapped and mailed directly from the store, be sure to indicate your recipient's name and address on

*Time is the most valuable thing a man can spend.*

Laertius Diogenes

your gift list to give to the store clerk. You can even make out a personalized card at home and have the store clerk include it in the box before he or she wraps the gift, so you don't have to spend extra time mailing the card separately from the present.

- Save time by doing your gift shopping on the Internet. Order books, candy, flowers, CD's, toys, and more in minutes—without leaving the comfort of your home.

- Can't think of what to buy for that person who has everything? Don't waste time or money trying to come up with something your recipient may or may not enjoy. Just get them a gift certificate to a major department store. They'll be able to choose what they prefer.

- Time is one of the greatest and most precious gifts to give. Instead of giving expensive gifts, consider simply visiting a friend or loved one for an hour, or a weekend.

- Hide gifts well so wandering eyes can't snoop, but make sure you jot down a note to yourself as a reminder of each hiding place. Keep this note in a secure place, such as a box with a lock.

- Don't waste time wrapping the gift yourself. Get it done in the store whenever possible.

- Keep the 3 P's of effective gift giving in mind:
  ❖ Planning
  ❖ Personalization
  ❖ Price

- Organize homemade gift baskets for family and friends. Here are some fun combinations:

Italian Dinner Basket: bottle of red wine, box of pasta, container of parmesan cheese, bag of mixed lettuce, bottle of Italian salad dressing, loaf of Italian bread, assorted imported candies.

Take Me Away Basket: relaxation audio-cassettes, bath salts, aromatherapy candles, lotions, assorted soaps.

Children's Birthday Basket: a few travel-sized games, a stuffed animal, some McDonald's Gift Certificates, a box of animal crackers, a bag of M&M's™, a book or video.

Housewarming Basket: pretty dish towels, oven mit, refrigerator magnets, copy of *Better Homes & Gardens Magazine*, potpourri, candles.

Especially For Him Basket: shaving cream, shaving lotion, a copy of *Sports Illustrated* and *TV Guide*, microwave popcorn, a video, a new tool.

*I say live, live,*
*because of the sun,*
*the dream,*
*the excitable gift.*

Anne Sexton

> *I have made this letter longer than usual because I lack the time to make it short.*
>
> Blaise Pascal

# Chapter 31

# Keeping in Touch

Our days are busy, but are they really too busy to keep in touch with people we care about? Or how about the people who can help us achieve our goals? Strive to manage your time so that you can keep in touch with the people who really matter in your life.

- Start an online networking forum—a.k.a. message board—to exchange ideas, tips, recipes and thoughts, rather than spending time on the telephone. Everyone can leave and read messages when convenient to them. It's more cost effective and less time consuming.

- Having trouble staying in touch with your good friends? Don't let them slip away. Schedule an appointment to call, write or e-mail them on a consistent basis. Work it out with them so that you contact them one month and they can contact you the next.

- If you have a computer, a great way to remember birthdays of friends and relatives is to use a reminder service. There are many free ones available online that e-mail you when the date arrives.

- Send an e-card and make someone feel great. There are many free e-greetings available that allow you to send your thoughts in minutes, without ever going to the store.
  Try http://www.bluemountain.com

- If you don't have time to write a long letter or note to a friend, a simple, 10-minute "how are you?" phone call will keep you in touch while saving time.

- Make a list of people you always send special occasion—birthday, anniversary, etc.—greeting cards to. Then, buy a year's worth of cards at the same time. You will definitely save time and you may be able to save money by buying in bulk. You can even address the cards the same day if you like.

- Buy additional, general greeting cards for unexpected occasions—birthday, anniversary, thank you, get well, graduation—in bulk so you'll always have them on hand.

- Don't have time for a long letter? A simple "Thinking of You" card may be all it takes to show someone how much you care.

- Host a barbecue or two each year. Invite your family and friends. You won't have to set individual dates with each person, but will still get to see everyone!

# Chapter 32

# Paper and Forms

An article I came across in the Wall Street Journal reported the average U.S. executive loses *six weeks per year* retrieving misplaced information from messy desks and files. The cost in salary and lost productivity is enormous.

Paperwork has been voted the biggest burden for businesses. Time spent mishandling paper detracts from the company's ability to service customers, increase sales and improve the bottom line.

It should never take you more than 10 seconds to find a piece of paper. If it does, then your office and file organization needs an overhaul.

- You can slay the Raging, Paper Beast with the **4 D's of Effective Paper Management**:

    ❖ **DO IT:** These papers require immediate action. Prioritize them and act on each today or tomorrow at the very latest.

    ❖ **DELEGATE IT:** These papers can immediately be delegated to someone else. Provide sufficient information so the person handling the actions knows what you expect.

    ❖ **DELAY IT:** These papers contain information that needs to be handled or referenced at a later date. Schedule a date on your calendar for any necessary action and file these papers away in a pending or archive file.

    ❖ **DUMP IT:** These papers have no value to you. Toss them in the wastepaper basket immediately!

- *"Handle any piece of paper once, and one time only."* I've heard this many times and firmly believe this advice is impractical for most people. Unless something is a complete emergency, I would never advise you to drop everything you're working on to do something that was just handed to you. However, keeping paper handling to a minimum is necessary. Every time you pick up a piece of paper, make a dot on it. Once there are three dots, you're probably just paper shuffling. The only way to really get the action completed is by scheduling a time to do it and acting on it.

- Sort it out. Before filing anything, sort through your piles and stacks. Categorize with the 4 D's. Don't file it if it's outdated or if it will be of no further use to you. 80% of what you file is never looked at again!

*The man who removes a mountain begins by carrying away small stones.*

Chinese Proverb

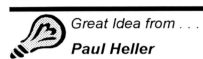

*Great Idea from . . .*
***Paul Heller***

*Do not wait to place important documents in your Tickler File (reminder file.) Put them in immediately, otherwise you may throw out an important document by accident.*

Paul Heller
Research Director, MGM Networks

- Eliminate paper clutter whenever possible. Instead of writing a physical note, send an e-mail. Save information on floppy disk or CD-rom, instead of on paper. Toss out the 10,000 Post-it™ notes living on your desk, bulletin board and walls.

  • Is a written note the best way to get your message across? Instead of adding to someone else's paper clutter, determine if a simple phone call or e-mail will do.

  • For those papers you're *truly* sentimental about—letters, cards, announcements—start a "Mementos File." Once the file is full, don't add anything else to it, unless you force yourself to replace one of the other papers in it.

  • Find a specific home for your important papers. Those papers that don't have a designated place will get lost. Either keep them in your Daily Action File, your Tickler or Reminder File, your filing cabinet or your Archive Files.

  • Don't let the paper in your in-box get out-of-control. Go through it a minimum of once a day and empty it out. It should be empty before you quit for the day and ready to receive tomorrow's papers.

  • If you're concerned about whether or not to keep a particular piece of paper, create a file called "Last Chance File," write the date it will be 30 days from today's date and place this paper inside. Each month, go through this file and throw out any papers past the date you indicated. If you didn't need it in the last 30 days, chances are you'll never need it again.

- Instead of reprinting copies of the same exact form or list from your printer every time you need a new one, keep a folder called "Master Forms." Print out your form once and place in this folder. Every time you need copies, just go to the file and pull it out.

- Make a form letter whenever you find you're typing the same information over and over again. There's no need to do the same work ten times!

- If you're writing the same information over and over again, create a standard form with checkboxes. It will save you loads of time.

- If you can't make your own forms for invoicing, tracking, hiring and more, buy prefabricated forms or computer software to help you out.

- Use two-part, carbon forms that allow you to *give a copy-keep a copy.* You'll save an extra trip to the copy machine or copy store.

- Keep large numbers of various forms in individual file folders or an accordion file. They'll be easy to retrieve when you need them.

## Paper Retention Guidelines

Can't decide if a paper should be kept or tossed? Here are some paper retention guidelines.

- Weekly or monthly salary statements can be tossed, *after* you check all items listed on your annual W-2 forms. Keep them in a safe place until then.

- Cancelled checks that relate to a specific item on your tax returns should be kept indefinitely.

- Medical bills should be retained for a minimum of three years.

- Expired guarantees and warranties can be tossed. While you're at it, throw out any instruction manuals for items you no longer have.

- Most mutual fund statements can be discarded. Keep only the consolidated annual report, which records transactions for the year.

- Credit card statements over a year old that have been paid can be tossed, unless there was a charge on one that relates to a specific item on your tax returns.

- ATM receipts that are more than a year old can be dumped.

- Old payment books from loans that are paid off can be dumped, as long as you have verification from the lender that your payments are complete.

- Warranty and guarantee related papers should be filed until the date has expired. Once the date is past, either attempt to renew your warranty or toss the outdated papers.

- The IRS recommends you keep your tax returns for at least four years after the date of filing, however you may want to be more conservative since these are vital government documents. Year to year tax returns take up very little room if they are nicely packed away in a few boxes and kept in a safe place. Those and other documents used to fill out your tax returns are your only defense in case of an audit.

- Newspapers over a day old are outdated and are of no use to you. Trash them today. Most magazines over three months old can be recycled immediately.

- Any papers that are outdated—the event already occurred, the information is no longer current—should be discarded immediately.

- Information on Post-it™ notes and business cards containing important names, addresses and phone numbers should be transferred to your database or address book. Don't keep hundreds of little pieces of paper. The same goes for those napkin notes too!

*The Three Rules of Work:*

*Out of clutter, find simplicity.*

*From discord, find harmony.*

*In the middle of difficulty, lies opportunity.*

Albert Einstein

# Chapter 33

# Filing System

Filing systems are indispensable for both your business and home life. No business or home should ever be without a filing cabinet and a good filing system. Since everybody has to deal with paper, and there's a lot of it, an effective filing system will allow for quick and easy paper retrieval whenever necessary.

There is no "one way" to file. Your filing system will always depend on your personal needs. However, the popular filing systems are:

✓ Alphabetical or alphabetically within categories (A, B, C, D . . . )

✓ Numerical or numerically within categories (1, 2, 3, 4 . . .)

✓ Chronological or chronologically within categories (Jan, Feb, Mar, Apr . . . )

Whichever you use, an effective filing system is one that allows you to find any paper you need in 10 seconds or less.

## Your Filing Cabinet

• Beware of the very inexpensive filing cabinets. They're usually nothing more than a nuisance, a hazard and a waste of money.

• Decide how many filing cabinets you need and what size. A small, two-drawer one may be fine now, but if you're going to accumulate more files in the future—and you probably will—buy a larger size. Try to project for the future and you'll save time and money.

• If the cabinet is too light, the weight of the files may cause it to tip forward when the upper drawers are open. Purchase a sturdy one.

• Be sure to buy the type of filing cabinet that can be converted from letter size to legal size and vice versa if necessary.

• Be sure to consider a design, style and color that you'll always be happy with. It will probably be in your office or home for years to come. In addition, consider a lock feature if you keep confidential files now or may in the future.

• Make sure the drawers of your filing cabinets slide in and out easily without a struggle.

• Filing cabinets aren't just for the office. They're perfect for home organization too. Keep all of your papers categorized and organized in a good quality cabinet. If you're going to leave it out in the open, you may want to consider one that has a nice wood finish to match your furniture. Otherwise, a sturdy metal one may do just fine. Make sure it comes with a system to hold, hanging folders. If it doesn't, you'll need to purchase one separately.

## File Drawers and File Holders

- Some desks conveniently have a large, built-in file drawer to keep everyday files. If you're lucky enough to have one, make sure it is designed to hold hanging file folders.

- If you don't have a desk with a file drawer for your everyday files, a terrific alternative is a free-standing file holder which can be placed at the corner of your desk or on a credenza that is within arms reach. Or, consider using an open hanging-file cart with wheels or a portable file carrier that can be kept under your desk.

- Label the *outside* of each file drawer. You won't have to open and close drawers to see what's in them. This is especially helpful if other people will be retrieving paperwork from your files.

- If you must keep your paperwork in binders, purchase hanging binders. This way, you can organize your papers in the binder. Then, simply hang the binder in your filing cabinet. Clearly label the spine of the binder, since that's what you'll see when you open your file drawer.

- When running more than one business or two divisions, use two separate filing cabinets or two portable file boxes; one for each business/division. Or, you may want to color code all the files for one business red and the other business green. The possibilities are endless, but the main point is if you're trying to keep everything in the same area, without any clear division, then everything is bound to get scrambled and disorganized.

## Your File Folders and Labels

- Your file folders should be crisp and new. Don't keep ragged, dirty, torn, decrepit file folders. They're messy and unprofessional. Old, ratty ones should go into your recycle bin.

- Before writing on your white file folder labels, first stick them to the manila file folder. Then write on them. You won't get marker or ink on your fingers when you affix the labels to the folders.

*Great Idea from . . .*
## Kathy Pankow

*I love having a filing cabinet at home. In addition to our household file folders, it's also great for filing interesting articles about lawn care, travel destinations and household tips.*

*I also file owner's manuals for purchases we make. Whenever we need to find one of these, we can get to them quickly. Plus, if we ever sell something, we could always pass the owner's manual on to the new owner.*

Kathy Pankow, Hubertus, WI

Kathy, a magazine merchandiser, is married to Paul, a systems technician for Ameritech. They have three children: Craig, Alissa and Ross.

- It wastes time to *type* labels for your file folders. By the time you walk over to the typewriter, insert a label sheet and find a folder to stick the label on, you could have been done already. Keep a few pre-labeled folders and simply write out your labels. You'll be done in seconds.

- Follow these tips for your *hanging file folders*:

  ✓ One color may work, but if you have a number of broad categories, such as Financials, Employees, Clients and Vendors, use separate colored hanging file folders for each category.

  ✓ Be sure to buy the proper size, letter or legal, depending on your needs.

  ✓ Make sure they come with clear, plastic tabs and inserts for labeling or purchase these separately.

  ✓ Always buy more than what you need right now. This way, you won't have to keep running back and forth to the store.

- Follow these tips for your "Manila Letter/Legal" file folders:

  ✓ You ask, "Why do I need manila file folders when I already have hanging file folders?" Well, you don't have to, but there are two reasons you may want to:

    ♦ Just use hanging file folders and in about a month (if not sooner) the papers inserted into them may begin to curl, settle their way down and get crushed.

    ♦ Hanging file folders are generally used for broad categories and manila file folders are placed into them for sub-categories.

  ✓ Since you can color code the hanging file folders, I usually recommend the manila file folders all in one color.

  ✓ Be sure to get the proper size manila folders, letter or legal, depending on your needs.

  ✓ A package of third-cut manila file folders—folders with alternating left, middle and right hand tabs—usually works best for quick viewing and easy retrieval.

  ✓ Use white labels and a medium-point black marker for labeling.

- Clear out your files when they're too thick to handle or every six months. Hang onto active papers. Dump anything outdated.

## Basic Filing System Tips

- Having a file folder labeled "Miscellaneous" is the kiss of death.

*You get credit for what you finish, not what you start.*

Anonymous

Miscellaneous files become nothing but catch-all files that have a 99.9% chance of never being looked at again. Every piece of paper that you *really* need to file can be categorized under a specific, descriptive, easy-to-locate file name.

- File new papers in your folders towards the front, so that your oldest material is always in the back. You won't have to waste time flipping through the entire file folder looking for the most current information.

- Don't keep overstuffed file folders. Once your categorized file folders have more than 50 or so sheets of paper in them, weed out what you don't need. If it's imperative that you keep everything in these folders—for legal purposes—you'll need to start a second file folder with the same category name. Label them, for example, Jones Account 1 of 2, Jones Account 2 of 2.

- Mark all papers with a discard date *before* filing them. The next time you go through your files, you can toss all papers that are past the date you indicated.

- Don't let your filing get out of hand. File immediately whenever possible. Otherwise, schedule daily or weekly filing appointments.

- Leave a "To Be Filed" holder on top of your filing cabinet to temporarily store papers until your designated filing date.

- Color code files for easier identification. For instance:
  ✓ Red for Urgent/Important Items
  ✓ Yellow for Client Files
  ✓ Blue for Employee Files
  ✓ Green for Financial Files

- Never use paper clips on the papers in your file folders. They catch onto other papers and cause misfiling. They also take up too much room. If you must attach papers together, use a staple instead.

- Create a "Filing System List" to jog your memory as to where you filed something. List the subject name, file drawer and file folder. This is especially helpful when other people will be in and out of your filing cabinet.

- Before you set up a new file holder with a new file category for a piece of paper, ensure that you can't file within a category you've already set up first. Be careful of starting too many new file categories that are going to do nothing more than confuse.

- Don't stuff large store or mail order catalogs into your filing cabinet. They take up too much space. Keep such material stored in a magazine box.

*Planning is bringing the future into the present so you can do something about it now.*

Alan Lakein

*We do more talking
progress than
progressing.*

Will Rogers

- If you have a piece of paper that can be categorized in two different folders and you're not sure which to use, file it in one. Then, cross-reference it on your Filing System List.

- When filing alphabetically, different people with duplicate names are filed: Last Name, First Name and then middle initial.

  *Example:*

  *Carlson, Jennifer*
  *Carlson, Jennifer M*
  *Carlson, Jennifer S*
  *Davidson, Mary*
  *Davidson, Mary F*

- When you have company names such as "The Home Store" or "The Supply Place" eliminate the word "the" in your filing system.

  *Example:*

  *Home Store*
  *Supply Place*

- When filing alphabetically, always file Last Name, before First Name.

  *Example:*

  *Anderson, James (not James Anderson)*
  *Lucas, Christine (not Christine Lucas)*

- When filing numerically, use actual numbers, not spelled out words. For example:

  ✓  *16*
  ✓  *17*
  ✓  *18 (not sixteen, seventeen, eighteen)*

- When filing in chronological order, you can file by:

  ✓  *Year (1999, 2000, 2001, 2002)*
  ✓  *Month (Jan, Feb, Mar)*
  ✓  *Date (3/1/99, 3/2/99, 3/3/99)*

  Or use a combination, such as filing year as the main category and month as the sub-category:

  ✓  *1999    Jan, Feb, Mar, . . .*
  ✓  *2000    Jan, Feb, Mar, . . .*
  ✓  *2001    Jan, Feb, Mar, . . .*

## Simple 7-Step Filing System

- This simple seven step system—that's quite the tongue twister, isn't it?!—can help you make and keep an effective filing system. Once done, you'll be able to keep your paperwork under control and find anything you need within 10 seconds or less.

  1) Categorize your information into the broadest categories possible. Think about your supermarket. They have specific areas for apples and oranges, eggs and milk, meat and poultry, etc. The 3 broad categories here are: Fruits, Dairy and Meats. The same goes for your paperwork. Some common categories are:

     Accounts Receivables
     Accounts Payables
     Clients A-H
     Clients I-P
     Clients Q-Z
     Prospects
     Employees
     Vendors
     Taxes

  2) Make hanging file folders for each of these broad categories. Make sure you use the hanging folders that are scored to hold tabs in a variety of positions.

  3) Then begin sub-categorizing with your manila file folders. For example, in your hanging file for Taxes, you may have manila file folders by year (one for 1999, one for 2000, one for 2001, etc.)

  4) Begin filing each piece of paper into the appropriate manila file folders. Mark each one with a discard date, this way when you go through your files a year from now, you'll immediately know if you should retain that particular paper.

  5) If you run into a piece of paper that could be filed in a few different folders and you're not sure which to file it in, file it in one folder and tape a cross-reference log to the inside of the other file. This will help you find it quickly later on.

  6) Allow several inches of play so drawers don't jam. Plus, if the drawers are too tight, filing is going to be a frustrating chore. And if it's going to be a chore, chances are, you won't do it.

  7) Once you have a good filing system together, file on a daily basis or at minimum on a weekly basis. If you let your filing get out of hand, you'll spend a lot of time getting it back on track.

**Great Idea from . . .**
**Chad Gracia**

*Label your file folders neatly and high on the tab at the top of the folder. That way, you'll be able to read your writing when the folders are full and the filing cabinet is stuffed.*

Chad Gracia
President of The Gracia Group

The Gracia Group is a consulting firm specializing in providing services to governments and businesses in the Middle East

http://www.graciagroup.com

## "Never Forget" Reminder System

- The "Never Forget" Reminder System is the perfect system for helping you remember items that need to be done, meetings that are coming up, events that are taking place and more! It's also wonderful for helping you plan when you'll begin working on tasks and projects. It automatically keeps you on top of those details and is very easy and inexpensive to set up. Here's how:

### Items Needed:

- ❖  12 Hanging File Folders with Index Tabs (one color)
- ❖  31 Manila File Folders (one color, but different color than the hanging ones. Third-cut.)
- ❖  31 White Labels for Manila File Folders
- ❖  1 Medium Point Black Marker
- ❖  1 Free-standing Hanging File Holder (This is optional. You can use your current filing cabinet for this system. However, many people like to keep the "Never Forget" Reminder System right out on their desk or credenza so they remember to look at it everyday.)

[1]  Take 12 hanging file folders and label their index tabs with Jan, Feb, Mar, etc. all the way up to December.

[2]  Place them in a hanging file holder on your desk or in your filing cabinet if you prefer.

[3]  Take 31 manila file folders (a different color than the hanging folders) and label them 1, 2, 3, 4, etc. all the way up to 31.

[4]  Place all 31 manila file folders in the hanging file for the current month.

[5]  As things come up that you need to do on a certain "day" of the current month, put a note in the folder for that day. If you need to start the item before a certain day of the month, put a note in the folder a number of days ahead of the date that it's due.

[6]  As things come up that you need to start in "another month," put a note in the hanging file folder for that particular month.

[7]  When the current month ends, the 31 manila file folders should be moved to the following month. Any notes that were in the hanging file folder for the month should be moved into their specific day folders.

[8]  Tack up reminders so you remember to look at your Reminder System every day at a specific time.

[9]  If you complete the activity, throw your note away. If not, put that note into your Reminder System again, either in another month, or in a specific day of the current month.

**Q.**  Where did the name "Tickler File" Come From?

**A.**  The "Never Forget" Reminder System is also known as the *Tickler File System*.

Legend has it that the name "Tickler" was also the name of a long feather commonly used by farmer's wives.

After spending long hours in the fields all week, the farmers were exhausted.

So when the farmers went to church services on the weekends with their wives, they'd constantly be nodding off.

The wives would bring along this long feather, called the Tickler, and tickle their husbands under the chin with it if they began falling asleep, as a "reminder" for staying awake.

Thus the term "Tickler" file was coined. It's a reminder for staying on top of our daily projects, tasks and activities.

## Filing System Categories

Categorizing is usually the one area in filing that is confusing for most people. The general rule of thumb is to always keep related or similar items together.

To make it a little easier for you, here are some common categories that can be used in any business or home filing system.

- **Office Filing System:**

| | |
|---|---|
| Accounts Payable | Accounts Receivable |
| Administration | Advertising |
| Articles | Clients/Customers |
| Company Policies | Company Goals/Plans/Strategies |
| Computer Related Tips and Instructions | Employees |
| Expenses | Human Resources |
| Legal | Operations |
| Project Files (Current) | Project Files (Future) |
| Public Relations | Reference |
| Research | Sales and Marketing |
| Tax | Training |
| Travel | Vendor Brochures/Information |

- **Home Filing System:**

| | |
|---|---|
| Automobile | Bank |
| Bills Paid | Camp |
| Children (one for each child) | Computer |
| Correspondence | Credit Cards |
| Decorating | Donations |
| Education | Entertainment |
| Finances | Home Improvement |
| Insurance | Legal |
| Medical/Dental | Property |
| Receipts | Religious |
| Rent/Mortgage | Repairs |
| Schools | Taxes |
| Travel/Directions | Utilities |
| Vacations | Warranties |

- **Vital Papers (should be filed in a fireproof box):**

| | |
|---|---|
| Birth Certificates | Citizenship Papers |
| Marriage Certificates | Adoption Papers |
| Divorce Decrees | Wills |
| Death Certificates | Deeds |
| Passports | Automobile Titles |
| Household Inventory | Veteran's Papers |
| Bonds/Stock Certificates | Vital Contracts (Lease, Patent, Copyright) |

*Folks used to be willing to wait patiently for a slow-moving stage coach, but now they kick like the dickens if they miss one revolution of a revolving door.*

Ed Wynn

Chapter 34

# Reminders and Lists

*Great Idea from . . .*

**Louise Block**

*As the owner and manager of a small business, I used to get upset when tasks like refilling the copy and fax machines were not completed. It's easy for employees to adopt the attitude, "It's not my job," or "I thought she did it."*

*Instead, we have developed a checklist of duties for each desk in our office. As we rotate work stations for a week at a time, everyone gets an opportunity to do all of the tasks on an equal basis. What's really great is that I never hear anyone complaining that the copy machine is empty, or "I filled it yesterday. It is her turn."*

*The completed checklists are turned in at the end of the week. In addition, a place for special projects completed is on the lists. It gives my employees a chance to note completed tasks that I may not have known about. Completing the checklists also gives each employee a chance to be recognized for her accomplishments.*

*We've had great success using our checklists.*

Louise Block
Block Business Call Center
1001 W Glen Oaks Lane, Suite 201
Mequon, WI 53092
(414) 241-2500

Kevin Trudeau created an audio course called *Mega Memory*. It's excellent and I highly recommend it. You'll be amazed at how well you'll be able to remember so many things after listening to his material and practicing.

Nevertheless, for years now, I've been using the most reliable memory system I know of. My mother taught it to me many years ago. She used to send me to the corner store to pick up a few groceries. Thankfully, she didn't just *tell* me what to buy. She knew I had other important things on my mind—like cartoons and chocolate ice cream!

To ensure that I wouldn't forget what she wanted me to buy, she made me a *list*. And guess what?! When I returned from the grocery store, believe it or not, I was able to remember everything on that list!

With all the things there are to remember these days, why would you ever commit anything important to memory alone? Always carry a paper and pen with you in case you need to jot something down. I guarantee this system. It works every time.

Then, get really fancy. For those things that you have to remember on a regular basis, create a checklist and make copies of it. For instance, if you are always forgetting what to do before you leave for a business trip, make a list of items you usually bring along with you. As you're packing, simply retrieve a copy of your list and check off each item as you put it in your suitcase. You're sure to remember everything you need!

• Create a "Master Office Supplies Checklist" and make copies of it as you need to. As you notice you're running out of staples, paper clips and other supplies, just check off the item that you need to replenish. Designate one day a week—or every two weeks—to buy or order necessary items.

• Reference lists are wonderful tools. Make reference lists for accessing information that you'd find useful and put those lists in an easy-to-access place. Jot down good ideas on your reference lists, as they come to you. This can save you hours. You won't have to waste time constantly looking things up or trying to remember.

- Here are some ideas for reference lists:

  ✓ Personal goals and dreams

  ✓ Birthday lists for business associates, friends and family

  ✓ Favorite restaurants with phone numbers

  ✓ Web sites you'd like to explore

  ✓ Books to read, movies to see, videos to rent

  ✓ Things to pack when traveling

  ✓ Gift ideas for friends, family and business associates

  ✓ Things you'd like to learn about

  ✓ A list of files in your computer directories

  ✓ A wish list of things you want to buy yourself

  ✓ Things you've lent to people and things you've borrowed

- When shopping for a major purchase, carry around a list of questions you need to ask. Jot down notes. It's easy to forget the details, especially when you have a variety of choices.

- Ever get all the way to work and realize you forgot to put on your wristwatch? That could be annoying. To avoid this from happening, make yourself a quick, morning checklist. Include anything you have to do before work—or school—and everything you must bring along with you.

- Tack up reminders where you can't possibly miss them; areas that are constantly in view. A note on your office door, telephone, mirror, car steering wheel or anyplace else that will catch your eye will help you remember all those details.

- If you're always oversleeping, it's time to kick the habit. Don't keep your alarm clock where you can easily reach over and turn it off. You'll probably fall asleep again. Place it at the far end of the room. This way, you actually have to get out of bed and walk across the room to turn it off.

- One trick many people use to ensure they wake up on time, is to set the bedroom clock anywhere from 20 minutes to one hour ahead.

- If you're on a tight schedule, you might want to put a clock in the bathroom. This will help you keep on track.

- To remember an upcoming concert, presentation or lecture that you're interested in attending, keep an "Events Folder" of the announcements you come across. Then, mark an RSVP date and the event date on your calendar. When the RSVP date comes around, decide if you really want to attend, and if so, look at the literature in your Event Folder and make any necessary reservations. Purge papers in this file regularly to keep it up-to-date.

*Great Idea from . . .*
**Scott Gracia**

*Write it down. If it's not written down, it's bound to be forgotten.*

*I use lists and Post-it™ notes as constant reminders of what I need to accomplish.*

Scott Gracia

Webmaster of . . .
"The Great Throwzini" Website

http://www.execpc.com/~miwave/throwzini.htm

- Use a tape recorder to instantly capture your thoughts and ideas. They work great in the car or if you have an idea in the middle of the night when the lights are off.

- Keep a pad and pencil by your bedside. If you have a flash of inspiration in the middle of the night, you'll be able to jot it down.

- Use triggering devices to alert you when you're not sticking to your priorities. A watch with an alarm or kitchen timer, set at half-hour intervals, works wonders.

- Do similar tasks every day at the same time. You'll get into the habit of knowing that when 3:00PM rolls around, you have to make your sales calls or when it is 4:45PM you automatically remember to tidy up your desk.

- Use the "Never Forget" Reminder System—described earlier in this book—to help you remember upcoming projects and events. Use it religiously and I guarantee you'll never forget!

- There are a number of memory techniques available such as pneumonics or memory by association. Your local library and/or bookstore has many books available on the subject.

- Use a computer program, such as Outlook™ or Lotus Notes™, to remind you when a deadline is coming up; or carry around a Palm Pilot™ to keep you on track.

---

### Great Idea from . . . **Judy Land**

*Use Post-it™ notes on the refrigerator for things that need to be done. Remove the notes, one-by-one, as each project/chore is completed.*

Judy Land
Sturgis, MI

---

## Your Master List

- Make a "Master List" of things to do. Look at it often.

- Always keep your Master List where you can see it and where it won't get lost under other paperwork.

- Use lined letter or legal size paper for your Master List. Never, never, never use scraps of paper . . . or napkins!

- There's no need to number items on your Master List. This is just a running inventory of things that need to be done. You'll be transferring your priorities to your To Do List.

- Don't waste time rewriting your Master List over and over again. Better yet, if you have a computer, make your Master List in a spreadsheet or word processing file.

- Each time you finish a task, draw a line through it. Or, if using a computer file, delete the completed item.

- If you don't use a computer to make your Master List, when your written Master List is 60% completed, transfer the unfinished work to another page and throw the old list out.

### SAMPLE CALENDAR AND TO DO LIST

**Today is Friday, 4/30/99**

- ❑ 10-11A Coach Jenette call, 555-5555
- ❑ 11:30-1:30P Hair appointment
- ❑ 2-4P Finalize newspaper column
- ❑ 4P Deadline for newspaper column
- ❑ Make bank deposit
- ❑ Order Mothers' Day flowers

---

### Future Items

**Mon........ 5/3/99**

- ❑ 10:30-11A Dr. Young re: office organization
- ❑ See Leslie to file amended tax return

**Tue......... 5/4/99**

- ❑ AIA's shipment due to arrive today

**Wed........ 5/5/99**

- ❑ 11A-12N Create new biz letter for Acme Glass

**Thu......... 5/6/99**

- ❑ FU every Thursday send Coach Jenette reminder
- ❑ FU with Kathleen re: meeting tomorrow
- ❑ 7-8PM Teleclass on Mentoring  555-5555

**Fri........... 5/7/99**

- ❑ 10-11A Coach Jenette call 555-5555
- ❑ 3:30-5P Londonderry-Kathleen meeting

---

### Completed Items

**Thu......... 4/29/99**

- ✓ 11A-12N Hudson-John Brown 2nd interview
- ✓ 7-8P Time Management Teleclass 555-5555
- ✓ Get rates to Jordan from Travel Network

**Wed........ 4/28/99**

- ✓ 2-2:30P Call newspapers to place ads
- ✓ 2:30-4P Work on newspaper column (due Friday)
- ✓ E-mail to AIA re shipment

**Tue......... 4/27/99**

- ✓ 1-2:30P Hudson interview with John Brown
- ✓ UPS shipment to AIA- ETA 5/4/99

**Mon........ 4/26/99**

- ✓ 10:30-11:15A Dr. Wallace re: new web site
- ✓ 11:30A Leave for Skyview Café lunch
- ✓ 12N-3P Lunch with multimedia group
- ✓ Letter to Taeko re: progress to date
- ✓ Back up my computer files
- ✓ FU call to Patricia re: summer schedule

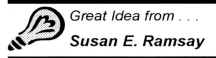

### Great Idea from . . .
### Susan E. Ramsay

*Keep your Calendar and To Do List together in a word processing document. Edit the document by adding new items, appointments and follow-up reminders. Move the yet-to-be-done items from yesterday to today's date—using cut and paste. Now you have your Calendar and To Do List for today in one document. Make sure the font size is 12 pts.*

*Take yesterday's Calendar and To Do List and reduce the font size to 8 pts. You can add items you did that were not on the list initially. This is a good way to keep track of (1) your accomplishments for performance review time and (2) phone numbers, etc., for future reference.*

*At the end of the year, you'll have a whole year's worth of appointments and accomplishments which you can refer to when you need to know (1) if they were done and (2) the date that they were done. Then it's time to start a new one.*

*I have done this with executives' calendars and To Do Lists that I am chartered to keep track of. It is a godsend. When working as an executive assistant at a company, I print out the executive's Calendar and To Do List every day and give it to him or her. I do not print out my own but constantly refer to it on my computer screen. That's one less piece of paper on my desk. When working in my home office for myself, I do print it out to take with me when I go out to see clients.*

*Future appointments can be kept below today's date and above the dates which have already passed. On my Calendar and To Do List, I have room for at least a week's worth, and sometimes a month's worth, of appointments and follow-up reminders.*

Susan E. Ramsay
Nashua, NH

Founder of Ideas & Solutions
Nashua, NH
Phone: 603-598-8699
Email: ramsay@gowebway.com
What's on YOUR To Do List?

# Master List

Make copies of this page and use it as your Master List or duplicate a similar form on your computer.

Make a running list of all the projects and tasks on your agenda. Don't worry about putting them in any particular order yet. Each day, simply choose items from this list and circle the appropriate priority code. Then, schedule them on your Daily To Do List. Once something has been transferred to your Daily To Do List, make a checkmark in the box. Once this list is 60% transferred, the remaining projects should be transferred to a new Master List.

A = High Priority (Important and must be handled today)

B = Medium Priority (I have to complete this, but it's not as important as A)

C = Low Priority (I may have to complete this, but it's not as important as A or B.) Note: If it doesn't really matter if you do it or not, it shouldn't be considered a *priority*. Reconsider whether it's even worth doing at all.

| Transferred to My Daily To Do List ☑ | Project or Task | Priority Code |
|---|---|---|
| ❑ | _____ | A    B    C |
| ❑ | _____ | A    B    C |
| ❑ | _____ | A    B    C |
| ❑ | _____ | A    B    C |
| ❑ | _____ | A    B    C |
| ❑ | _____ | A    B    C |
| ❑ | _____ | A    B    C |
| ❑ | _____ | A    B    C |
| ❑ | _____ | A    B    C |
| ❑ | _____ | A    B    C |
| ❑ | _____ | A    B    C |
| ❑ | _____ | A    B    C |
| ❑ | _____ | A    B    C |
| ❑ | _____ | A    B    C |
| ❑ | _____ | A    B    C |

# Daily To Do List

Make copies of this page and use it as your Daily To Do List or duplicate a similar form on your computer.

Using your Master List, choose today's projects and tasks. Choose a maximum of 3 High Priority items and 2 Medium Priority items. If you are able to complete all of these today and have time left over, it's your choice if you wish to add another item to today's list or take a break. Once each item is completed, check it off on your list. Move anything incomplete to tomorrow's Daily To Do List.

Today's Date is _____

**Completed**

☑

**"A" Priority Projects or Tasks**

❑ _____

❑ _____

❑ _____

**"B" Priority Projects or Tasks**

❑ _____

❑ _____

**Additional Projects or Tasks (if all of the above are completed)   Priority A or B or C**

❑ _____

❑ _____

❑ _____

❑ _____

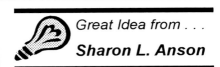

## Great Idea from . . .
### Sharon L. Anson

*I helped a friend develop a "Plan of Action" when she was feeling overwhelmed. The basic concept was: Attack it one step at a time.*

- *Break each task down into 15-30 minute increments:*

  *Wash the dishes.......... 15 min*
  *Do laundry................. 30 min*
  *Pay bills.................... 20 min*
  *Complete form .......... 20 min*

  ***Total Time ............... 85 Min***

- *Pull together anything necessary to complete each job so there's no delay in beginning or a reason to stop.*

- *Do each task one at a time. Stop when the 15-30 minutes are up, even if not completely finished. Put that task aside and continue on to the next task. Carry over anything not completed to the next day.*

*To her amazement, she was completing more tasks than ever before without feeling overwhelmed!*

*As for myself, a single mom with two very active boys (ages 8 and 14), I find this method allows me to get everything completed in a STRESS FREE manner with flexibility, which leaves me time for myself or activities with the boys (Friday night is Monopoly night!)*

Sharon L. Anson
Springfield Gardens, NY
Sha Designs
(Custom Home Decorating)

## Chapter 35

# Planning and Scheduling

In order to effectively manage our time we must plan and schedule. Just having a list of Things To Do isn't enough. It doesn't give a clear enough picture. Some of the items on that list will have to be prioritized to the top of the list. Certain projects have deadlines attached. Other things may depend upon other people, while some may rely upon information that you're waiting for.

- The 3 P's of effective time management are:

  ❖ **Planning** (plan the who, what, when, where and how)

  ❖ **Priorities** (put the important tasks at the top of the list, discard those tasks that are meaningless)

  ❖ **Pacing** (break the task down into smaller pieces, regulate the time needed for each section)

- Take a few moments every day to prioritize. Everything is certainly not a life and death emergency.

- Don't waste time attempting to prioritize 1,000 different things. Choose the important ones. Discard the rest. Then, put them in order.

- Control your day by planning it. Stay on schedule with a timer or a watch with an alarm.

- There's a very fine line between *high-standards* and *superhuman* expectations. Take a moment to determine if you could *really* complete a task to your satisfaction by the date that you've scheduled.

- Don't wait until you wake up to look at your calendar. Look at it the night before so you know what's coming up. Then, just glance at it in the morning to double-check your schedule.

- Pad your time when scheduling. If you think something is going to take 15 minutes, schedule a half-hour for it. In doing so, if you're running late, the rest of your schedule won't be thrown off. Better yet, if you're running early, you'll be able to start something else or take a break before your next task.

- Consider using one of the many software programs that can help you automatically track meetings, appointments, birthdays, anniversaries, events and more. Many programs offer a built-in alarm clock that will sound off when you should leave for your meetings and appointments.

- Do similar tasks at the same time each day. Having a consistent schedule will make it easier for you to remember what needs to be done. For example, if you have to make sales calls, plan to make all of them each day between 4:00-5:00PM. If you have to file, plan on filing every Friday at 3:00PM.

- For most people, the tasks and activities they perform every day do not drastically change. If you have consistent activities from day to day, an Action Schedule with no more than 4 vital tasks and 4 other tasks per day, can help you keep on track without getting frustrated. This form can be created on a computer using any word processing or spreadsheet program.

- If you're always running late, set your watch ahead 15 minutes.

- When waiting for a web site to load, or basically when you're waiting for most anything, don't just sit there *and wait*. Do something productive with your time. Read a quick letter. Jot down an important note. Tidy up your desk.

- When scheduling, plan to use your most productive time to do your most productive work. You may be at your best, first thing in the morning or perhaps later in the afternoon. Either way, it makes more sense to tackle your most difficult and important work at the time of day when you're most alert and most likely to complete it accurately. You're sure to double your work output.

- Get the worst over with first. As a child, I always ate my asparagus first. Once it was gone, the rest of my dinner was enjoyable. Do the difficult jobs first and the rest will be smooth sailing.

- Set 10 minutes aside every morning to look at your schedule and determine what needs to be done.

- Set 10 minutes aside every Friday afternoon to review what you have accomplished and to scan next week's schedule so you know what's coming up.

- Sandwich the tasks you don't like to do in between the ones you enjoy doing. Alternating back and forth will help you finish those tasks you're not thrilled with, because you'll constantly be looking forward to doing the tasks you enjoy.

- The more you complain, the longer it will take to finish. Determine if it really needs to get done and if it does, find an easier, less stressful way to complete it.

- Avoid doing something a certain way, just because someone else is

*Scheduling is the fine art of packing every day "just full enough" of the most useful activities.*

*Too full and you're liable to exhaust yourself.*

*Too loose and you're wasting precious time that can be used to work towards your goals.*

Anonymous

doing it that way. First, ensure it's the most efficient way. If it isn't, devise your own strategy. On the other hand, if someone is already doing something very efficiently, don't recreate the wheel. In other words, copy the best and discard the rest.

- Make it a rule to stop working at a particular hour—for example: every night at 6:30PM—to ensure you have plenty of time to do the things you love to do. Don't take any business calls after your designated time either. Let your answering machine pick up and you can then get back to your callers in the morning.

• Don't try to juggle too many things at once. You're bound to start losing things, miss deadlines, add to your stress and leave a lot of loose ends.

• Don't get caught up in trivial tasks. One wasteful activity usually leads to another and before you know it, you haven't spent any time at all on the important stuff.

• Most people underestimate the time it takes to do a given job. For the average person, things take twice—or three times—as long as anticipated. Pad each project by 15 minutes or more.

• Break your projects and tasks down into smaller, bite-size pieces that can be accomplished within a shorter span of time. This way, you can schedule your time to work on a variety of projects and still accomplish what you need to.

• Get out of bed a half-hour early to organize your thoughts for the day.

• Don't schedule creative, deep-thinking work for times when you know there will be interruptions.

• Let people around you know what your priorities are. Post these priorities in a visible place, such as a bulletin board or message area. This way, people will be aware and will be less likely to waste their time or yours with trivialities.

• If you are easily overwhelmed, it may be best to give your full attention to one project, instead of many. This will ensure you start and complete each project.

• Always save up your easiest tasks for the end of each day. You'll be able to complete them and end each day on a positive, rewarding note.

• Remember to plan and schedule time for the things you love to do. Saying, "I'll get around to it when I'm less busy," will most likely result in *you never getting around to it*. Schedule specific dates and times for yourself and fun activities and keep those appointments when the dates arrive.

*Great Idea from . . .*
**Kathy Harshman**

*I have a couple of daily rituals that help keep me organized. First of all, I use the "Today" section of my daily organizer diligently. I write in everything from the day's appointments to class assignments, or tests that my children will need my assistance on. At the end of the day I can see what I have accomplished and I add the tasks that were not completed to the next day's list.*

*This also helps me not to procrastinate. I will most likely fulfill a task if it has been on my list for a couple of days, even if it's something I dread doing.*

*Secondly, I set time aside each day to go through the mail and the papers that the kids bring home from school. Important papers are filed, and junk thrown out. This keeps it from piling up and overwhelming me at the end of the week.*

Kathy Harshman
Clearwater, Florida
Wife and mother of two children.

Kathy's Designs
http://www.kathydesign.com
Professional Web Design
For Home Businesses

## Chapter 36

# Your Calendar and Planner

J ust as it's important to schedule and plan your projects and activities, it's also necessary for you to write this schedule down. Just relying on your memory is not enough. You will end up forgetting something important.

This is where your calendar, day timer or planner comes into play. As you determine what needs to be done, it should immediately be scheduled on your calendar. Many people only write down tangible things, such as writing a report or attending a meeting. However, you can also schedule time to think, to set goals for yourself or to read an article that you've been meaning to get to.

*I've been on a calendar, but never on time.*

Marilyn Monroe

- Never use more than "one" calendar. Use one calendar for both business and personal use. Heed the old Chinese proverb, "A man who wears two watches never knows the correct time." If you keep one calendar in your briefcase, another on your desk, and another on the kitchen refrigerator, you're guaranteeing that something scheduled on one will never get written on the other.

- Use the FILI technique with your calendar. First Item, Last Item. In other words, when you get to the office, the first item and the last item for that day, should be to look at your calendar.

- Plans are meant to be improved. The goal is not to create a plan and stick to it, but to create a plan and ask the question, "Is this still working?" When your answer is "No," it's time to revise the plan.

- Purchase the right planner for your needs. Make sure the lines are large enough for your handwriting. Ensure the pages are big enough for you to fit all your important tasks.

- Use a calendar that displays an entire week or month at a time, rather than just a day or two. You have to look into the future to be able to make time for projects, goals and enjoyment.

- The first entry in your calendar or planner should be:

*If lost, please return to:*

*Name_____     Address_____*

*Phone_____*

*Reward $10 (or whatever amount you feel you'd be willing to give in the event of loss.)*

- Check your daily planner every day, hence the name *daily planner*. If it isn't checked religiously, something will be missed or forgotten.

- There is no need to use *every* planning page that comes with your daily planner. Decide which pages will help you the most and pull out the ones that you'll never use.

- Don't plan your projects, tasks and activities on scraps of paper, Post-it™ notes or napkins! There's a 99.9% chance that those papers will get lost.

  - When you schedule something, immediately jot it down on your calendar or planner. This way, all of your information will be recorded in one easy-to-locate place.

  - If you're constantly running around from appointment to appointment, or travel frequently, consider trading in your *loose* address books, appointment books, To Do Lists and calendars for a single planner that does it all and more. You can purchase very professional and fashionable ones from Franklin/Covey or Day Timer, or opt for less expensive, less fancy ones at office supply stores.

  - When shopping for a planner, here are some things you might want to look at in order to make the right choice for you:
    ✓ One that opens up and lies flat, so you can easily write in it
    ✓ A zipper closure so you don't lose anything
    ✓ A calculator, or pocket to hold one
    ✓ Address Pages with room for e-mail, voicemail, fax and pager notes
    ✓ Calendars
    ✓ Business card holder
    ✓ Diskette or CD-rom holder
    ✓ Attractiveness—one you'll be proud to carry around
    ✓ Size—one that meets your requirements
    ✓ Color-coded tabs so you can easily find each section
    ✓ Post-it™ notes holder or a notepad for quick notes
    ✓ Compartment for maps
    ✓ Pockets for receipts and loose papers
    ✓ Zip pockets for pens, paper clips and other supplies

- Instead of indicating a meeting, birthday or other event on your calendar by writing out the entire word, save some time by abbreviating common events. For example: MTG for meeting, BD for birthday, PU for Pick up, FU for Follow up and VAC for vacation.

*Great Idea from . . .*
*LaNita*
*Filer-Jones*

*Use a pencil to schedule events in your daily planner. You can then easily adjust for items that need to be cancelled, changed or rescheduled.*

*Simply erase, rather than writing in pen or marker and your planner won't end up looking messy and disorganized.*

LaNita Filer-Jones
Professional Organizer

Organizing Concepts Plus
8880 Bellaire, Ste 176
Houston, TX 77036
(713) 777-2254
(713) 779-8789 (Fax)

- Make an appointment with yourself at the end of each December to buy a calendar for the new year. Transfer regular yearly events from the old calendar to the new one immediately. Mark consistent dates, such as birthdays and anniversaries, with brightly colored markers so you'll be able to see those events coming up at a glance.

- Don't scramble at the last minute searching for where you put those tickets for the ball game, workshop or theater. When you mark the event on your calendar, also jot down where you put the tickets. A few days ahead of time, put the tickets in an envelope and tape them to the inside of your front door or on your light switch so you immediately see them as you're leaving.

- When using a calendar that you don't keep open constantly, use bookmarks on the most frequently used pages so you don't have to flip through the book each time. Don't use a pen to hold your place. It will destroy the binding and your calendar may fall apart before the year is up.

- Use stickers, a highlighter or different colored pens on your calendar to categorize different events. For example, highlight your meetings in yellow, birthdays in blue, reminders in orange and project deadlines in green. You'll be able to quickly scan the page without having to read your notes.

- If you're on the road often, a Palm Pilot™ may be a good choice for you. They hold addresses, To Do Lists, calendars, virtual notepads and more! They're a bit pricey, but are perfect for keeping the frequent traveler organized.

- Instead of bringing your entire calendar on the road with you, just make a photocopy of the page—the entire month—and bring that copy only. You'll have less to carry. Plus, there won't be any chance of losing your calendar.

- If your company's computers are set up on a LAN—local area network—using software such as Microsoft Outlook™ is a great tool. Everyone can fill in their own personal schedule for everyone else to see. Let's say you want to set up a meeting but are not sure when everyone will be available. Outlook allows you to view everyone's schedule right on your computer, without having to contact a single person individually. It's a real time saver and a great planning tool.

- When you come across an event that you'd like to attend, such as a seminar or a festival, immediately write the event name, place, time and any other appropriate information in the appropriate day on your calendar. Don't wait to do this. Time flies and you'll forget about it if it's not written down on your calendar.

*Great Idea from . . .*
**Lance Flanagan**

*Don't leave your planning until the last minute. Always write down everything you need to do tomorrow, the night before.*

*I use my day timer for this purpose and it works beautifully. I always accomplish everything I set out to do.*

Lance Flanagan, Boulder City, NV

Lance is married to Jean.

He is the Western Zone Manager for Abicor Binzel.

# Weekly Time Log

Make copies of this page and use it as your Weekly Time Log or duplicate a similar form on your computer.

This Weekly Time Log will allow you to determine exactly what it is that you're working on all week. Keeping track of your time allows you to get an entire picture of what you're doing. This way, you can make decisions as to what to eliminate, determine what needs to be streamlined and ensure you're spending enough time on your important goals.

Create codes that represent your activities, such as M for Meeting, or P for Presentation, etc.

Week of _____

| Time | Sun | Mon | Tue | Wed | Thu | Fri | Sat |
|------|-----|-----|-----|-----|-----|-----|-----|
| 7:00a | | | | | | | |
| 7:30a | | | | | | | |
| 8:00a | | | | | | | |
| 8:30a | | | | | | | |
| 9:00a | | | | | | | |
| 9:30a | | | | | | | |
| 10:00a | | | | | | | |
| 10:30a | | | | | | | |
| 11:00a | | | | | | | |
| 11:30a | | | | | | | |
| 12:00p | | | | | | | |
| 12:30p | | | | | | | |
| 1:00p | | | | | | | |
| 1:30p | | | | | | | |
| 2:00p | | | | | | | |
| 2:30p | | | | | | | |
| 3:00p | | | | | | | |
| 3:30p | | | | | | | |
| 4:00p | | | | | | | |
| 4:30p | | | | | | | |
| 5:00p | | | | | | | |
| 5:30p | | | | | | | |
| 6:00p | | | | | | | |
| 6:30p | | | | | | | |
| 7:00p | | | | | | | |
| 7:30p | | | | | | | |
| 8:00p | | | | | | | |

# Education and Entertainment Planner

Make copies of this page and use it to schedule time for educational or entertainment reading, programs, trips, etc. or duplicate a similar form on your computer.

Simply fill in each event under the appropriate month. Indicate the specific day. Cross out events as you complete them. Reschedule events you don't get to do on your scheduled date. Create your own Event Codes for those not listed.

**Event Codes:**

R=Read          W=Watch Program/Video          L=Listen to Audio          T=Go on a Trip

__ = _____          __ = _____          __ = _____          __ = _____

### January

Day   Code   Description

_____
_____
_____
_____
_____
_____

### February

Day   Code   Description

_____
_____
_____
_____
_____
_____

### March

Day   Code   Description

_____
_____
_____
_____
_____
_____

### April

Day   Code   Description

_____
_____
_____
_____
_____

### May

Day   Code   Description

_____
_____
_____
_____
_____

### June

Day   Code   Description

_____
_____
_____
_____
_____

### July

Day   Code   Description

_____
_____
_____
_____
_____

### August

Day   Code   Description

_____
_____
_____
_____
_____

### September

Day   Code   Description

_____
_____
_____
_____
_____

### October

Day   Code   Description

_____
_____
_____
_____
_____

### November

Day   Code   Description

_____
_____
_____
_____
_____

### December

Day   Code   Description

_____
_____
_____
_____
_____

*In order to succeed you must know what you are doing, like what you are doing and believe in what you are doing.*

Will Rogers

# Chapter 37

# Telephone

It's amazing, but when you think about it for a moment, the telephone can be a major time saver or a major time waster. However, it really has nothing to do with the phone itself. As you already know, the telephone is one of our greatest inventions. The truth is, whether it saves or wastes time depends entirely on you.

Organize your incoming and outgoing phone calls and you'll guarantee that every call you make or take will be an effective use of your time.

- Designate a specific hour each day to be used as your "Telephone Hour." This is the time that you can return your phone messages, make your important calls, track down information and keep in touch with people all in one concentrated burst.

- Leave answering machine messages that either require no reply or are very specific about what you need and when. Make sure you always leave your name, number and the best time to reach you. This will help to avoid unnecessary phone tag.

- Cordless telephones are great. You can talk and do something else at the same time in any room and outside.

- Use a stopwatch or timer to time your calls and keep you on track.

- Take notes while you're on the phone. It will help you to remember important items, dates, events and questions. Don't try to keep it all in your head.

- Most phones have a speed dial feature. Program the numbers you call frequently to save time when dialing. You also won't have to waste time looking up numbers!

- Most phones now come with an automatic redial feature. If the line is busy, it will keep redialing for you automatically. Just don't wander off too far!

- Buy long phone cords, so that you can talk on the phone and do something else across the room at the same time.

- Instead of answering the telephone whenever it rings, consider screening your calls by letting your answering machine take the calls for you. Every interruption you have while trying to get a task completed increases the time it takes to do so.

- Make a list of mindless tasks that you can do when you're on the telephone and keep this list right by your phone. As you're talking, you can do any of these items. Remember to make sure it's a mind-less task, such as sticking stamps on envelopes. Otherwise, you won't be able to really pay attention to your caller and any impor-tant information they're trying to relay to you.

- Get yourself Caller ID. It will identify your callers and you can de-cide if you want to take the call or not.

- Get a million telemarketing calls? When a telemarketer calls, ask them to remove your name from their list immediately. Federal law requires them to honor your request for removal. In addition, you can write to the Direct Marketing Association's Telephone Prefer-ence Service and register your name/number as a "Don't Call.":

Telephone Preference Service
Direct Marketing Association
PO Box 9014
Farmingdale, NY 11735-9014

- Only have a few moments to talk? Place a time limit on your in-coming phone calls. Say, "I've only got 5 minutes to talk."

- Long-winded answering machine announcement messages are an-noying to your callers. Make them as short, but as descriptive, as you can. Tape your script to the bottom of the answering machine in case it accidentally gets erased.

- Ask someone to screen calls for you. Employ an answering service. Use voicemail or an answering machine.

- If you're out and you know you have to make a call when you re-turn, but don't want to forget, call your answering machine and leave yourself a message. Make it a habit to check your answering machine as soon as you get home, or arrive back at the office. Buy one with a loud, annoying beep that keeps going off until you check your messages.

- Instruct callers that can be serviced by others to contact those qual-ified people directly.

- Help your assistants help you. Create a written list of which callers should be put through and which shouldn't.

- Prioritize your calls. Schedule a specific time for each.

- Ensure that calling is the best first step. It may be more efficient to send out written material first.

- Have a clear idea of what you need to say and have all materials pertinent to the call in front of you. Make a list of items that have to be communicated, so you don't forget something.

> *All time management begins with planning.*
>
> Tom Greening

- Communicate via e-mail or notes whenever possible to avoid telephone tag.

- Rather than leaving a message if your call recipient isn't available, leave your name and the time you'll be calling back with the receptionist or on the recording. In doing so, you're more in control and you'll eliminate the possibility of your caller calling back and missing you once again.

- Create and use a Visible Phone Message Center so that you have an open and organized *temporary* area to help keep track of your phone messages and to get you to act on them in a timely manner. Here's how:

[1] Hang a corkboard labeled "Phone Message Center."

[2] Divide the board into 2 with a strip of colored tape right down the middle.

[3] Label one section "Critical." Label the other "Non-Critical."

[4] Stick 5 push pins in the "Critical" section, and 15 in the "Non-Critical" section. Not everything is critical. There will *always* be more "Non-Critical."

[5] Provide your staff with pink phone message slips and inform them that all messages are to be placed on the Phone Message Center in the appropriate section. Messages left elsewhere will be disregarded. Make sure you tell them what constitutes "critical." A "critical" message is one that will cost the company dearly if it's not responded to immediately.

[6] Respond to your "critical" messages as soon as you see them on your board. Throw these messages out when the action is completed. No sense in keeping an extra piece of paper.

[7] Respond to your "non-critical" messages as follows:

✓ Schedule a time that day to return the calls that you can. Throw the messages out when the action is completed.

✓ For any call that can't be returned that day, schedule a future date and time in your calendar to respond to those messages. Throw the messages out as soon as they have been transferred to your calendar.

[8] Record any new phone data in your Rolodex and throw the message slips away.

- Don't be afraid to write in your free Yellow Pages or White Pages phone book. Highlight numbers with a highlighter. Correct listings that have changed. Place a star next to restaurants that you enjoy. Doing so will save you scanning time in the future.

## Chapter 38

❖ ❖ ❖ ❖ ❖ ❖ ❖ ❖ ❖ ❖ ❖ ❖ ❖ ❖ ❖ ❖

# Mail

Even though you're probably familiar with and using e-mail on a regular basis, we still rely on snail mail more than ever. Besides the US Postal Service, we also depend on Federal Express, UPS, Airbourne Express and others. There are even mailing services that we use. Mail Boxes Etc. is one of the popular ones.

Yes, even though we're living in an electronic world, snail mail is here to stay. I'm a heavy e-mail user, but I still enjoy opening the mailbox and receiving a letter, a package, a greeting card—anything but a bill!

I know. You may be saying how much you hate to receive junk mail. Well, there are a few things you could do to ease up that load. Plus, there are quite a few things you can do to make your mail sending and receiving duties easy and effective.

- Is your mailbox overflowing? You can try cutting your junk mail a bit by writing to the following address and asking them to add you to their "Don't Send" list:

  Mail Preference Service
  Direct Marketing Association
  PO Box 9008
  Farmingdale, NY 11735-9008

- Type a quick "Please remove me from your mailing list" note with your name and address on it. Make copies of it. Then, whenever you receive a piece of junk mail, send a copy of your "Remove Me" letter back to that company.

- As soon as the mail arrives or at your designated time each day for going through your mail, sort it. Don't let it pile up. Do it before your next mail delivery.

- Keep personalized name and address self-stick labels in your briefcase or purse. They will save you a minute or more each time you have to write out your name and address on a form, coupon, subscription and contest entry.

- If time is very limited for you and your budget isn't, you may want to try a mailing service, like Mail Boxes Etc. It costs more for them to pack and apply postage, but the lines are generally shorter than the post office and it will save you tons of time.

- A great way to take care of incoming mail questions that can be

*I enjoy writing in the desert. There are no distractions such as telephones, theaters, opera houses and gardens.*

Agatha Christie

answered immediately is to hand write a note on the original letter and mail or fax it back immediately. In many cases, there's no need to take the time to type a formal note back.

- Create your own Mailing Station. Include:

  ✓ Postage for whatever denominations you regularly use

  ✓ Postage meter

  ✓ Current list of postal charges—available from the post office

  ✓ Zip code chart

  ✓ Mailing paper

  ✓ Strong mailing tape and scotch tape

  ✓ Mailing labels

  ✓ Envelopes (letter size, large sized, bubble filled)

  ✓ Forms for special mail (registered, certified, priority, Fed Ex)

  ✓ Stapler/staples/staple remover

  ✓ Pens/markers

  ✓ A wet sponge (unless everything is self-stick)

  ✓ Assorted stamps ("date", "handle with care", "fragile")

- Since a large portion of mail can be immediately tossed, open your mail over the trash can.

- If you are constantly mailing things out, gather 100 envelopes, 100 stamps and 100 return address labels. Pre-stamp and pre-label the envelopes so they're ready to go when you need them.

- When you order something through the mail, keep a copy of the original order form, or tear out the page from the catalog. Reference important notes such as the ordering date, the company's name/address, how you paid and the date the item is supposed to arrive. Place this information in a "Mail Order" file folder. Make an appointment with yourself to check this folder every few weeks. When the product arrives, check it against your ordering information for accuracy. Then, do one of the following with the original ordering information:

  ✓ toss the information away if you're sure you're going to keep the item

  ✓ date it and keep it in a "Toss in 10 Days" file, just in case you may need to send the item back

  ✓ date it and keep it with your tax information if you need it as proof for your accountant

- Have envelopes pre-printed with your return address on them, whether used for business or personal.

- Buy yourself a postage scale and pick up a rate card from the post office. You'll know exactly how much postage should be applied without having to make extra trips to the post office.

- Want to know how much something is going to cost to mail without having to make a trip to the Post Office? Check out the neat rate calculator on the US Postal Service website:

  http://www.usps.com

- Keep a list of US state codes nearby. When you need to send something out-of-state, you'll have a handy list to reference.

- Store a stack of Express Mail forms and envelopes in your office if you use these services regularly. You can get everything together—everything packed, forms filled out—before you drop it off.

- Save a trip to the post office and order your stamps by mail or fax.

- Don't buy just a few stamps at a time. Buy at least 100 or more and reduce frequent visits to the post office.

- Designate a mail basket for Incoming Mail. Whenever the mail arrives, just place it in the box until your scheduled time rolls around for sorting the mail.

- Don't let your incoming mail get out-of-hand. If there is more than a day's worth of mail piled up, it will take much longer to sort.

- Designate a mail basket for Outgoing Mail. Whenever you have something to mail, just toss it inside. Then, instead of going to the post office every day, just go once a week.

- Use self-adhesive stamps. Why would you want to use the kind that you have to lick?

- Instead of licking envelopes to seal them, get the self-stick kind. If they are outside of your budget, use a water squeeze bottle with a sponge—designed specifically for this purpose—or a glue stick. This is especially helpful and time saving if you have to seal a volume of envelopes.

- Avoid going to the post office during work day lunch hours, Saturday mornings or the days right before the holidays. The lines are generally very long and you'll waste an hour or more waiting.

- Buy blank postcards from the post office that already have postage on them. You'll have a postcard ready to go when you need one.

- Use a stamp holder that dispenses self-stick stamps from stamp rolls. They begin the peeling for you.

- Purchase a postage meter if you send out a great deal of mail. These are great for small and home businesses.

*Activities with clearly defined goals and deadlines are those activities that will get done.*

Anonymous

> *Time goes you say?*
> *Ah no!*
> *Alas, time stays;*
> *we go.*
>
> Austin Dobson

# Chapter 39

# Office Space, Supplies, Equipment

Keeping your office organized is a matter of continuous improvement. Are you staying on track? Survey your office a minimum of once a week. If you answer "No" to any of these questions, you're not making the most effective use of your space and it's time to organize.

✓ *Can I find everything I need, when I need it?*

✓ *Is my office free of piles and other obstructions?*

✓ *Are each of the items in my office functional?*

✓ *Am I making effective use of my wall space?*

✓ *Do I have enough breathing room to work comfortably?*

- Organizing tools can help, but don't be under the misconception that any organizing tool or product can get you organized on its own. Many people believe that a helpful product will automatically organize them. It's simply not true. A great set of golf clubs may "help" you improve your game, but they will not take the place of dedication and practice to learn how to use them properly. The same is true of organizing tools.

- Use clear, plastic, hanging, shoe organizers with divided pouches. They can be hung over a door and are excellent for storing paper clips, stamps, rubber bands and other office supplies. Find them in dollar stores, mail order catalogs and home furnishing stores.

- Measure, measure, measure. Then measure once more. Don't ever purchase equipment or furniture before careful measuring. Make sure you leave breathing room. Avoid blocking air ducts. Make sure you have enough room to reach electrical sockets

- If you have room to store office supplies, you may want to buy them in bulk. You may be able to save money in volume discounts by doing so, plus you'll eliminate unnecessary trips back and forth to the office supplies store.

- Always losing your pens? Why not try a mounted coil pen. These have adhesive backing and stretch cords that can be mounted on your desk or telephone.

- How many times have you set trash down on your desk because there wasn't a trash can right there? Or because the little, teeny one you do have was overflowing? Keep a *large* wastepaper basket in your office *right near your desk*. This way, you'll be able to dump your junk mail and other trash immediately.

- If you don't have a specific place for your daily supplies, they will get lost. Desk caddies sit on your desk and generally have 4+ different sized compartments that conveniently hold your favorite pens, pencils, scissors and other daily supplies.

- Dump your pens that are out of ink and your pencils that have shrunken to minuscule bits. Sharpen your usable pencils!

- Keep your own reference library—dictionary, thesaurus, almanac, style and grammar book—on your credenza or on a nearby shelf. This will allow you quick look-up capabilities. If you're online, you won't need the books. Lots of reference can be done online and for free, without taking up any desk or shelf space.

- Affix lucite wall pockets to your wall. Clearly label each one to identify the contents. If you deal with a number of different people, buy more than one, in various colors. Assign one to each person.

- Get your reference books off your desk. Install wall shelves for them or get a bookcase.

- Attach large, erasable planning calendars to the wall. Everyone in your office will know your schedule without having to ask you.

- Roll-away and portable office carts can be stocked with office supplies and other necessary items and stored out of sight. They come in all shapes and sizes so you can make use of those tight spaces that are usually left unused.

- Get a sturdy filing cabinet for your filing needs. And remember, your filing cabinet is not the place for shoes, purses or your lunch. Think of it as *high-rent space* to be used for the specific purpose of filing away your most important papers.

- Unless you're a frequent business traveler, you may not need an expensive, leather planner. Three-ring binders are excellent for holding all your planning tools—To Do List, Calendar, Schedule, etc.—and are a fraction of the cost.

- Use floppy disk and CD-rom holders. They'll keep disks off your desk and handy when you need them.

- Use vertical file sorters, baskets and other organizing tools to organize your files and incoming/outgoing papers.

- Your most important pieces of office equipment are probably going to be your computer and printer. Don't skimp here. Purchase a computer with extensive memory and high speed capabilities. Buy a high-speed, high-resolution printer.

*The standardization of time is the basis of a classificatory system that rules life. Except for birth and death, all important activities are scheduled.*

E. Hall

# Office Supplies Checklist

Make copies of this page and use it as your Office Supplies Checklist or duplicate a similar form on your computer.

Simply add in any supplies not already listed. Then, check off each item as you're running low. Bring this list to the store with you to ensure you remember to purchase everything that is needed.

## Desk Supplies

___ Pens
___ Pencils
___ Markers
___ Highlighters
___ Paper Clips
___ Scotch Tape
___ Rubber Bands
___ Erasers
___ Stamp Pads
___ Ink for Stamp Pads

## Filing Supplies

___ Manila File Folders
___ Hanging File Folders
___ Pocket Folders
___ File Labels
___ Index Dividers
___ Tabs

## Binding Supplies

___ Staples
___ Bulldog Clamps
___ Fasteners
___ Glue
___ Glue Sticks
___ Reinforcements
___ 3 Ring Binders 1"
___ 3 Ring Binders 1 1/2"
___ 3 Ring Binders 2"

## Paper Products

___ Spiral Notebook
___ Writing Pad
___ Post-it Notes
___ Phone Message Pads
___ Stationery
___ Laser Printer Paper
___ Copy Paper
___ Fax Paper
___ Graph Paper
___ Colored Paper
___ Pocket Notebook

## Supplies for Hanging

___ Pushpins
___ Thumbtacks
___ Map Pins

## Computer/Printer Supplies

___ Toner Cartridges
___ 3.5" High Density Disks
___ CD-Roms
___ Zip Drive Tapes

## Time Tracking Supplies

___ Calendar
___ Refills for Planner
___ Time Cards
___ Scheduling Forms
___ To Do Lists

## Identification Supplies

___ Price Tags
___ Name Badges
___ Wide Labels
___ Colored Circle Labels

## Stationery/Mailing Supplies

___ Letterhead/Second Sheet Letterhead
___ Business Cards
___ Letter Envelopes
___ Catalog Envelopes
___ Padded Envelopes
___ Shipping Paper
___ Shipping Labels
___ Disk Mailers
___ Bubble Wrap
___ Sealing Tape

## Other

___ _____
___ _____
___ _____
___ _____
___ _____

## Chapter 40

# Fax and Copy

Sending and receiving faxes is not a luxury for most businesses. Rather, it's a necessity. For the information that can't be sent immediately via the internet, the fax machine is the next best thing.

Just because the fax machine is useful, however, does not mean it's totally self-sufficient. It takes an organized person to change the paper when necessary, to make sure incoming faxes aren't landing all over the floor or curling up like scrolls and to make sure all faxes are sent without transmission errors. The same effective organization is necessary for the copy machine.

Whether you work in a small, home-based business or a large Fortune 500 company, getting organized with your fax and copy machine will ensure that you use your equipment productively.

*In the modern industrial age, the key machine is not the steam engine, but the timepiece.*

Jacques Attali

## Fax Machine

- Prepare and make multiple copies of your own fax transmittal cover sheet to use when sending faxes. It should include:

  ✓ Your name, company name, phone number and the current date

  ✓ Space for your recipient's name and company name

  ✓ Space for you to indicate how many total pages, including the cover sheet, are being sent

  ✓ Check boxes for you to mark an appropriate action that you'd like your recipient to take—Urgent, Reply ASAP, Please Comment, Please Review, For Your Information.

  ✓ Space for you to write your message

- If you use a computer, you can design your fax as a type-in form, instead of having to write out your fax correspondence. Plus, you can store common fax numbers and program a formula into it so that the date appears automatically.

- For those faxes that don't require a long cover note, use small, adhesive "Fax it" notes instead. These small notes, which include your name and your recipient's name, are simply stuck on the paper you're faxing. There's no need for a cover sheet. You'll save fax transmission time and paper.

- Put fax supplies near the fax machine—cover sheets, a pen, fax paper, extra toner and copy paper—so they're handy.

- Make sure your fax machine has something to catch incoming faxes in or they'll end up all over your floor.

    • Use a fax program on your computer. Send a file directly from your computer without using a single sheet of paper and without wasting time walking to the fax machine.

    • Use a fax machine that automatically redials when the line is busy. You won't waste time waiting for the line to free up.

    • Program common phone numbers into your fax machine. Instead of having to remember and dial manually, you can send with the press of "one" button.

    • Keep your fax manual close to the fax machine for future trouble-shooting or for answers to questions, otherwise you're going to waste time searching for it.

## Copy Machine

• The copy machine has made the paper duplication process so quick and easy. Be careful you don't let this simplicity result in copies that aren't really necessary, thus wasting time and generating paper clutter.

• For those forms that you use every day, instead of making one copy at a time, make a number of them. You won't waste time going to the copy machine a hundred times.

• Don't make a million copies and freely distribute them to *everyone* without first determining if they really need them. You'll be contributing to someone else's paper clutter.

• Put copy supplies near the copy machine—extra paper, toner, paper clips, staples—so they'll be handy when you need them.

• Whenever possible, use a copy machine that has helpful functions such as collating and stapling capabilities.

- Purchase paper that is already pre-3-hole punched. Feed this paper into your copy machine first, instead of using regular paper and then wasting time punching holes later.

- Keep your copy manual close to the copy machine for answers to questions you may come across, otherwise you're going to waste time searching in the future.

- Keep extra toner and fax paper on hand. Don't let it run out unexpectedly and cause frustration, stress and wasted time.

*Great Idea from . . .*

***Chad Gracia***

*Don't save paper copies of things that are available on the Internet. Unless you don't have easy access to the web, or if you like to hold scraps of paper in your hand, there is little reason to collect standard recipes, general information on clients/competitors, or news items.*

*Most of these can be found within seconds on the Internet, and so the time spent categorizing and retrieving paper copies may be better spent.*

Chad Gracia
President of The Gracia Group

The Gracia Group is a consulting firm specializing in providing services to governments and businesses in the Middle East

http://www.graciagroup.com

# Chapter 41

# Addresses & Business Cards

While helping Jennette—a client—get her office organized, she pulled out six shoeboxes full of business cards and little papers with names and addresses she'd been collecting for years. Since she didn't know what to do with them, they would simply be tossed into one of these boxes. Jennette wanted suggestions on how to organize them.

I asked her "When was the last time you opened up one of those boxes to find a name?" She replied, "Are you crazy? I've never tried to find someone in one of those boxes. I'd be sitting here sifting through the box all day!"

She agreed that she would probably *never* use the cards in those boxes. So, I had her bring each box over to her trashcan and dump them out. She liked this solution and was happy to get rid of the business card clutter.

Then, I helped her devise a plan to transfer necessary business card information into her database immediately.

- Never keep a business card that you'll probably never use again. Toss it out immediately.

- Get a Rolodex™ card file to hold names and addresses of your contacts, or use your computer to store these names.

- Clean out your Rolodex™ or computer address file periodically. Remove people who you haven't spoken to in a year or more and especially people you don't remember.

- If you use an address book, use a pencil or erasable ink when making entries. Erasing is neater, plus it eliminates the need to have to run out, buy a new address book and rewrite the entire book over again when you're out of space.

- Better yet, keep addresses/phone numbers in virtual space on your computer. It's much easier to make revisions and saves time. A database serves this purpose well.

- Invest in a cardpunch for your business cards. Instead of manually transferring information from your business cards to your Rolodex™, just file your cards in your Rolodex™ instantly.

- Don't waste your time and energy with colored, plastic Rolodex™

*There are only two sure ways to fail. You either quit, or you don't start.*

Anonymous

card covers. They take up too much space and waste time when you need to make an adjustment.

- If you must keep a number of business cards, use a business card book with plastic sleeves. Designate a page for the A's, a page for the B's, etc. Only keep the business cards of people you really need. Go through your business card book periodically. Purge outdated cards and those that refer to people who you'll never contact again.

  - Pull business cards and Post-it™ notes with names and phone numbers off of your bulletin board. Enter new or updated phone numbers into your Rolodex™ or computer file right away.

  - Don't waste time *typing* each Rolodex™ card. Simply hand write the information needed.

  - Tape business cards to the Rolodex™ card; there's no need to spend time copying over the information.

  - Organize Rolodex™ cards or your computer card file database alphabetically by company name or last name of contact.

  - Don't keep hundreds of blank cards in your Rolodex™. They take up too much space. Keep a few blank cards in the back and store the rest with other office supplies.

  - Use the back of your Rolodex™ cards to record important information about the person or company indicated on the front. Information such as agreement/serial numbers, spouse's or children's names and more can be very beneficial to have on hand.

  - Use a computer database for all your names and addresses. Whenever you want to do a mass mailing, you'll be able to print out labels instantaneously and effortlessly.

  - If you are going to benefit by keeping a particular business card, either place it in your Rolodex™ or copy it into your computer database. If you are not going to benefit from it, dump it as soon as you get back to the office or when you get home. Most of us take business cards in the first place, purely out of politeness.

- Store your personal business cards in the box they came in. Keep them in your supplies cabinet. You might want to keep a few in your wallet or organizer in case you need one on hand.

- If clients visit your office, you may want to pick up a business card display holder. Place it at the end of your desk facing your visitors so they can take one with them if they desire.

- Get really organized and use your business cards as sales tools. In addition to printing your name, company and address information on the front, have a special offer or discount printed on the back!

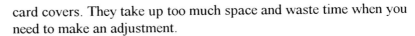

 *Great Idea from . . .*
***Lillian Kaufman***

*Use an empty box—business card size—to collect business cards from meetings, shows and other events. Write the name of the event and the date you attended on the back of the card before you include it in the box. At a later date, schedule time to add these cards to your mailing list.*

Lillian Kaufman
When you think of Jewelry,
Think of "Diamond Lil"
http://www.diastarjewelry.com

# Chapter 42

# Your Desk

When was the last time you saw your desk? If it has been awhile, today is the perfect day to find it under those towering, paper mountains. You ask, "How long will it take?" Well, the time is dependent on the size of the desk, the amount of papers on it and the time you last remember seeing the surface. However, I estimate that it will take a minute or two to clear it off, and anywhere from 1-8 hours to dump the unnecessary stuff and reorganize everything else.

## Organize Your Desk in 12 Simple Steps

[1] Schedule at least 4 hours for the first half of this mission. When the day arrives, dress in sweatpants and a t-shirt—you know, ultra-comfortable. Play your favorite music in the background and take a deep breath.

[2] Get ready. Get set. Go! Take every last thing off your desk, and out of your desk. Place it in a big pile on the floor. You're done clearing off your desk. See, I told you it would only take a minute or two.

[3] Scrub your desk with disinfectant and then furniture cleaner until it looks shiny and new.

[4] Get a large trash bag, have a seat on your floor and begin dumping. Over 80% of the papers on your desk can probably be trashed. This includes your day timer from 1975, the 20,000 business cards you come across, the brochures from that seminar that took place over 5 years ago. The only things you should keep are your active projects, papers to be referenced in the future and anything you must keep for legal purposes. Ok, and maybe another piece of paper or two that you can't bear to part with. When you see something that meets one of these criteria, place it in a pile behind you.

[5] It's probably time to grab another large garbage bag. Maybe two or three more. But keep dumping. You're doing great!

[6] Next, begin tossing old newspapers, magazines and catalogs. Most are probably outdated by now, but even if they aren't, they will be over the next day or two. Again, if you see one or two that you desperately want to keep, that's fine. Just don't keep forty-two!

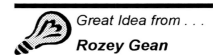

*Great Idea from . . .*
**Rozey Gean**

*While I can't stipulate that having my desk organized, causes me to relax, I can vouch that it helps me to maintain FOCUS. Without all the extra junk on my desk, I can focus better on the job in front of me.*

Rozey Gean
Founder of WEON
Women Entrepreneurs
Online Network

FREE Membership.
Visit: http://www.weon.com

[7] Now you're down to those final items that are not paper, old calendars, business cards, newspapers, magazines or catalogs. This includes that old, grimy coffee cup, random office supplies, pocket change and some widgets that you can't even identify. Three words: TOSS! TOSS! TOSS!

[8] Time for lunch. Go out and get something to eat. Go for a walk. Escape your desk for at least an hour. You deserve it! While you're out, purchase a fresh pad of paper, a pen/pencil caddy, a vertical file holder—unless you have a drawer that fits hanging file folders—for the files you use every day, some fresh manila files—with hanging file folders if you'll be hanging your everyday files—and labels, and a holder for your computer disks and CD-roms if you don't already have one.

[9] When you return, it's time to reorganize the stuff you're keeping. Hopefully, it's just a very small pile. Most of the things from your desk should probably be in the trashcan. Categorize and organize your everyday files into your new folders. Label each clearly. Place these folders in your brand new vertical file sorter. Those papers that are not your everyday papers should go into your filing cabinet —this is assuming you already have an effective filing system set up. If not, place these papers in a basket on top of your filing cabinet and read the section in this book on setting up a filing system.

[10] Place your telephone back on your desk, along with your computer if you have one. Your new, fresh pad of paper should be placed near the telephone. Set up your new pen/pencil caddy and place some supplies inside—throw out those pencils that have shrunken to miniscule bits and those pens that don't write. If you have room for some office supplies in your desk, designate one of the drawers and place them inside. If not, supplies should be placed in a supplies cabinet. Your planner—this year's only—can now be placed on your desk.

[11] Ok, we're in the finishing stretch! Anything else you've come across that you haven't tossed, but I haven't mentioned above, should probably not be stored on or in your desk. Computer manuals belong on a shelf in your office, not your desk. Set up your computer disks and CD-roms in the new holder you just bought. Place them next to your computer. Photographs? Put them in frames and hang them on your wall. Random widgets? You don't need them. Throw them out.

[12] Congratulations!! You must feel great. You deserve a dinner with a scrumptious dessert! Why not reward yourself tonight? Read on for some additional tips to keep your desk looking neat, clutter-free and organized. Make a solemn vow. Promise yourself never to let your desk disappear again. Good work!

*Nothing is worth more than this day.*

Goethe

- Keep a *large* wastepaper basket in your office right near your desk. This way, you won't have the opportunity to start accumulating junk on your desk again .

- Eliminate random paper piles and classify your papers by categorizing them into open desk trays and baskets. Make sure each tray and basket is clearly labeled as to what should be placed in them.

- Set up an In Basket for your incoming projects and an Out Basket for your outgoing projects. These can either be placed on the end of your desk or on a nearby credenza. Apply the 4 D's of Effective Paper Management to the items in your In Basket, so you can empty it by the end of each day.

- Use vertical file sorters on your desk to hold daily and frequently used file folders.

- Store supplies such as pens, pencils, Post-it notes, scissors and a stapler in an organizing caddy on your desk, or in a compartmentalized tray within your desk.

- Instead of taking up your desk space, hang your framed pictures, photos and other inspirational items on the wall.

- Separators for the insides of desk drawers keep all items in their own designated place.

- If you have a computer on your desk, get an attachment for the keyboard so it can be stored underneath and pulled out when needed.

- Space saving, drop leaf, wall mounted desks and tables are great for saving room. Use them in your small office or home office.

- Schedule at least 15 minutes at the end of each day clearing off your desk. Don't leave your office unless you've done so.

- Outlaw anyone else placing anything on your desk. Set up a Lucite wall pocket or an In Basket for incoming projects and other paperwork that you must look at. Tell them that if they leave it on your desk, it's going in the trash can.

- The only paperwork on your desk should be the project you're working on right now. Everything else belongs in folders in your file holder or filing cabinet until you're ready to work on it.

- If you're right-handed, keep the telephone on the left hand side of your desk, and vice versa. You'll be able to hold the receiver and write at the same time.

- Begin each day with a clear desk and a clear mind. A clear desk is *not* the sign of a sick mind. It shows that you're organized, professional and you have respect for your surroundings.

*The man who starts out going nowhere, usually gets there.*

Dale Carnegie

> ### You miss 100% of the shots you never take.
>
> Wayne Gretzky

# Chapter 43

# Down to Business

Whether you own your own business or work for someone else, establishing organized systems is essential to the success of your career and company. All aspects of a successful business, including marketing, advertising, customer service, billing, finance, human resources, employee management and more require an organized approach.

- If you send the same letters, brochures and price lists to prospects and clients when they request it, make your packages ahead of time. Enclose all necessary information in your packets and store them away until you need them. This way, when somebody asks for your materials, the packets will be ready to go.

- Keep information on your contacts, leads and customers current. A database is the perfect tool for keeping everything organized and up to date.

- Create form letters for routine correspondence you are writing and re-writing again and again. Make copies and you'll have instant responses to common inquiries.

- Tag your necessary follow-ups in your calendar or reminder file.

- Follow up with your clients and customers on a regular basis. Schedule follow up phone calls and visits with them. Write these appointments on your calendar to ensure everything is running smoothly and to determine if they need anything else from you or your company.

- Create standard "Reminder Forms" to send to clients and customers when a scheduled appointment is coming up or when the product they purchased is due for service.

- Use a checklist to help you remember all of the necessary steps in your sales process.

- Send invoices out to your clients on the same day each month. For example, January 26, then February 26, then March 26, etc. Your clients will know exactly when to expect your bill and you won't get confused as to whom you've sent a request for payment.

- Keep on top of payments received from your clients. If someone misses a payment, immediately send out a friendly reminder. Don't let too much time pass. You'll waste hours agonizing over how difficult it's going to be to collect payment.

- Instead of writing and re-writing collection letters to clients whose payments are past due, create four standard collection letters. Then, simply type the person's name and address on the letter and send it out:
  - ✓ First: friendly reminder
  - ✓ Second: 30 days past due
  - ✓ Third: 60 days past due
  - ✓ Fourth: final notice before forwarded to a collection agency

  To receive 4 standard Collection Letters, ready for you to use, send a self-addressed, stamped envelope, along with a check or money order for $ 5.00 to: Collection Letter Request, Effective Business Systems, PO Box 240398, Milwaukee, WI 53223-9015.

- Create an Employee Policy Manual if your company has employees. There won't be any question about the policies you've set. You won't be asked the same questions over and over again. In addition, you'll have proof of policies in case you need it for legal purposes.

- Create detailed checklists for your employees to follow. They'll always do the projects you give them exactly as you want them done and they won't forget the steps since they'll be in writing.

- Hold weekly meetings with your department managers to keep on track of projects and goals in individual areas of your business. Always have a planned agenda with goals.

- Create two company newsletters:
  1) An Employee Newsletter will:
     - ✓ provide employees with current company info
     - ✓ alert employees to company events and contests
     - ✓ motivate them by congratulating them for accomplishments and promotions
  2) A Customer Newsletter will:
     - ✓ provide customers with current company info
     - ✓ alert your customers to special offers and discounts
     - ✓ keep you fresh in your customers' minds

- Always set goals and deadlines for everything you're trying to accomplish. Doing so will set you in the right direction and, with the right tools and motivation, you're sure to succeed in whatever you set out to do.

---

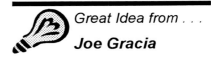

**Great Idea from . . .**
**Joe Gracia**

*"Marketing is everything you do to attract and keep customers."*

*To help attract the greatest number of customers at the lowest cost, it's vital to know exactly which marketing efforts are winners—they make you money—and which ones are losers—they lose you money.*

*You can easily do this with a simple tracking system.*

*Assign a code to every marketing piece you use—ads, flyers, post cards, sales letters, press releases, etc. The code can either be a fictitious Extension Code next to your phone number (Ask for Ext. 215), or a fictitious Dept. Code in the address line (Dept. MJ215 = Milwaukee Journal Ad, February 15th).*

*By simply asking your prospects for the code number, you can keep an accurate response tally for each marketing effort on a one page log. Now you can invest more in what's working and eliminate what isn't.*

Joe Gracia, Brown Deer, WI

Joe is my loving husband and business partner. He helps business owners grow their businesses through the use of effective marketing systems and tools.

For a Free Marketing Idea Kit:
Call: 414-354-5891 Ext. 215

or write to:

Free Marketing Idea Kit
Effective Business Systems
PO Box 240398 - Dept. FO215
Brown Deer, WI 53223-9015

# Prospect Contacts and Results

Make copies of this page and use it to track your Prospect Contacts and Results or duplicate a similar form on your computer. You should have a specific goal and result for each prospect you call or meet. Use this form to help you keep track of all communication with prospective customers.

◆ Contact Name_____    Date_____
Goal_____    Result_____
_____    _____
_____    _____
Follow-up Action_____    Follow-Up Date_____

◆ Contact Name_____    Date_____
Goal_____    Result_____
_____    _____
_____    _____
Follow-up Action_____    Follow-Up Date_____

◆ Contact Name_____    Date_____
Goal_____    Result_____
_____    _____
_____    _____
Follow-up Action_____    Follow-Up Date_____

◆ Contact Name_____    Date_____
Goal_____    Result_____
_____    _____
_____    _____
Follow-up Action_____    Follow-Up Date_____

◆ Contact Name_____    Date_____
Goal_____    Result_____
_____    _____
_____    _____
Follow-up Action_____    Follow-Up Date_____

◆ Contact Name_____    Date_____
Goal_____    Result_____
_____    _____
_____    _____
Follow-up Action_____    Follow-Up Date_____

◆ Contact Name_____    Date_____
Goal_____    Result_____
_____    _____
_____    _____
Follow-up Action_____    Follow-Up Date_____

# Marketing Goals and Results

Make copies of this page and use it to track your Marketing Goals and Results or duplicate a similar form on your computer.

You should have a specific goal and result for each prospect you call or meet. Use this form to help you keep track of all communication with prospective customers. Use additional codes for marketing activities not already listed.

Activities:

| | | | |
|---|---|---|---|
| DM=Direct Mail | AD=Ad | NR=News Release | PS=Presentation/Seminar |
| EW=E-mail/Web | T=Telemarketing | R=Radio | TV=Television |
| __ = _____ | __ = _____ | __ = _____ | __ = _____ |

| Date | Activity Code | Detailed Description | Number of Leads | Number of Appointments | Number of Sales |
|---|---|---|---|---|---|
| | | | | | |
| | | | | | |
| | | | | | |
| | | | | | |
| | | | | | |
| | | | | | |
| | | | | | |
| | | | | | |
| | | | | | |
| | | | | | |
| | | | | | |
| | | | | | |
| | | | | | |
| | | | | | |
| | | | | | |
| | | | | | |
| | | | | | |
| | | | | | |
| | | | | | |
| | | | | | |
| | | | | | |
| | | | | | |
| | | | | | |
| | | | | | |
| | | | | | |
| | | | | | |

> *Counting time is not as important as making time count.*
>
> James Walker

# Chapter 44

# Especially for the Home Office

Running a business from your home takes a bit of creative thinking, especially when you live in a small home or apartment. Whenever possible, it helps to have a separate room in your home which you can consider your office. If you don't have an additional room though, you have two choices:

A) Designate a section of your home for your business activities.

B) Make your office a portable one—one that could be rolled or carried into the closet when you're not doing business.

Besides the space problem, there's also the distraction dilemma. At home, there are many possible distractions. Chores seem to call your name from every direction. Children demand your attention. The television or radio is beckoning. Personal phone calls keep coming in.

There are things you could do though, to get organized and make your home office one that helps you get down to business and achieve your business goals.

- Define your home office space, even if your office is a corner of the family room or kitchen. Keep all office-related items in one place to create an efficient central spot and eliminate wasted time looking all over the house for things you need.

- Set up your home office with the same basic tools used in larger businesses. You'll probably need a desk, supplies—pens, paper clips—filing cabinets, phone, organizing baskets and a computer.

- Folding screens are decorative and disguise a work area, without having to put everything away when you're expecting guests.

- It's easy to get distracted when working at home. Announce that your office is off-limits to family members while you're working.

- Designate separate supply storage areas for family members, so that they won't *borrow* your office supplies.

- Never work within earshot of the television. You'll be distracted and you won't be able to concentrate on your projects. Wear ear plugs if you have to or close your office door.

- Don't allow yourself to take phone calls from friends and family members during business hours, unless it's an emergency. Just because you're home, doesn't mean you're not working.

- Many home businesses run into the problem of their personal mail getting mixed up with their business mail. To avoid this, create two in-baskets; one labeled Personal Mail and the other labeled Business Mail. As soon as the mail arrives, or at your designated time each day for going through your mail, sort it immediately into one of these two baskets.

- Many times people are more productive when they're dressed for success. Instead of working in shorts and a T-shirt, try dressing up as if you're about to attend an important meeting.

- If you work out of your home, be sure to keep your business papers separated from your personal papers. Keep them in two separate filing cabinets, or at minimum, in two separate drawers of the same filing cabinet.

- Roll-top desks hide all paperwork you're not using right this minute from view. Desks with flip-up panels serve a similar purpose.

- Consider designating an entire room for your office if possible. A guestroom or den may work well. If you simply don't have the space for this, use a computer cart and a rolling file cart that can be stored to the side or in another room if you're expecting company.

- For home offices on the go, create a portable office to keep in your car. Get a portable container that holds letterhead, envelopes, paper, pens, a calculator, business cards and other necessary supplies.

- Store your files in portable crate systems. When you "close shop" for the day, you can just put your office files in a closet, under the desk or somewhere out of the way.

- You need a filing cabinet to organize your paper. If you're going to be keeping it in a prominent place, consider purchasing a wooden one that blends in with your other furniture.

- Be careful to always back up your computer files, especially if your computer is used by both you and other family members. One wrong slip by someone and you're liable to lose all the work you've put so much time into.

- When you work in a home office, you can easily lose track of the time. Set a scheduled quitting time, otherwise you may be working until the wee hours of the night.

- Have multiple phone lines installed in your home; one for personal, one for business, another for your fax machine and another for your computer. With all the wonderful and time-saving technology these days, there shouldn't be anything holding you back from making the most out of your business, especially a lack of phone lines.

*Time is what we want most and what we use most.*

William Penn

# Chapter 45

# Travel and Driving

Save time, money and energy by getting organized whenever you travel, whether you're traveling to the grocery store or to another country. Make your journey as stress-free as possible. Accomplish everything you set out to do.

- For places that you visit periodically, keep directions in a file folder labeled "Directions." This way, you won't have to waste time asking how to get to the same place more than once.

- If you travel a lot, you may want to consider a cellular phone for emergencies. Better to be organized and safe, than sorry. *(Side note: Just please, don't talk on the phone while you're driving. It's a hazard to you, your passengers, cars, pedestrians and animals on the road.)*

- When commuting, make good use of your time. Listen to motivational or instructional tapes. If you're a passenger, you can even bring your laptop computer along to type up a letter or read a book.

- Don't travel anywhere without a Swiss army knife. They usually include a paring knife, scissors, nail file, screwdriver, bottle opener, toothpick, tweezers and more. You never know when you'll need a quick and handy tool.

- Before traveling for business or pleasure, orient yourself to your destination area before you leave. Read travel books, take a look at a map, contact the Chamber of Commerce. A little planning could make your trip much more enjoyable.

- Maps older than a year or two can be outdated. If you have maps from places you visit infrequently, toss them and obtain new ones later when needed.

- Travel to the beach frequently? Get a beach bag and fill it with your beach accessories—hat, visor, sunglasses, a towel, suntan lotion, headphones, plus a list of any last minute items you may need. This way, when the mood arrives, you'll be all packed and ready to go.

- If your job allows, ask to telecommute from home one day or more per week. This will reduce time, gas, clothing costs and wear and tear on your automobile.

*Great Idea from . . .*
**Michael Pisano**

*Always keep a spare car key in your wallet. If you accidentally lock your keys in the car, or even worse, lose them, you'll have a spare on hand.*

Michael Pisano, Jersey City, NJ

Michael, my Dad, is married to my mom, Margie. They have one other daughter; my sister, Jude.

- Make a checklist of all items you need when you travel. Make copies of this list and put them in a labeled travel file. Whenever you need to go on a trip, just pull out a list and check off items as you pack them away.

- If you travel with your family, make a travel list for each family member. Keep these in a travel file folder.

- Never leave packing for the date of your trip. Pack at least a day ahead of time. Use a checklist to ensure you take all necessary items.

- If you can't carry your luggage effortlessly for one full block, you have too much in your bag. Lighten your load.

- Booking your vacation through a good travel agent, instead of doing it by yourself, may save time, offer you additional incentives and ensure everything was booked properly.

- If you enjoy arranging your vacation on your own, consider booking your vacation online. You won't have to spend time driving to a travel agent or making telephone calls.

- Leave copies of your itinerary with people who can reach you in case of an emergency. If for pleasure, be sure you define what you consider to be an emergency. People have a funny way of making *everything* an emergency, even when it's not.

- When traveling internationally, exchange your money for the local currency before getting to the airport whenever possible. The lines at the airports are usually much longer.

*Great Idea from . . .*
**Jean Flanagan**

*Always keep a hand held tape recorder in the car.*

*If you have an idea while you're driving or want to jot something down, that's obviously tough to do when you're trying to keep your eyes on the road.*

*Simply record. The detail you want to remember will not be forgotten.*

Jean Flanagan, Boulder City, NV

Jean is married to Lance.
They have two dogs named Bailey and Cody.

## Traveling by Car

- Don't be caught on the road without an organized emergency kit in the trunk of your automobile. Include a flashlight—with an extra set of batteries, a first-aid kit, an extra can of oil, a container filled with water, windshield wiper fluid, a snow scraper/brush, a lock de-icer, a tire inflater, paper towels/moist towelettes, jumper cables, items for changing a spare tire and flares.

- Join an auto club such as AAA or another roadside service club. These services are life-savers for emergencies or for those of us who really don't want to take the time or energy to change a tire or who are dressed too nicely to do so.

- Don't waste hours driving in circles. Whenever in question, pull over and ask for directions or look at a map.

- Wondering how long it's going to take you to get somewhere?

Divide the miles in the trip by the miles per hour, generally the speed limit minus 5. The result will be your driving time. (Example: **125 trip miles** divided by **55 mph minus 5** will result in approximately **2.5 hours of driving time.**)

- Spend lots of time in the car? While you should always have your driver's license and car registration in your possession, your glove compartment can hold your other essentials:

  ✓ insurance card

  ✓ maps

  ✓ tissues

  ✓ sunglasses

  ✓ car manual

  ✓ list of towing/repair services

  ✓ your AAA card

  ✓ pen/pencil/paper

  ✓ extra $10 for a quick fuel refill (just in case)

  ✓ vital phone numbers

  ✓ discount coupons for car wash/oil change

  ✓ a change purse with spare change

  ✓ a flashlight

  ✓ driving gloves

- If you use your car for business purposes, keep a mileage record in the glove compartment and record your miles after each trip.

- If you declare a "No eating or drinking" policy in your car, you'll spend less time cleaning crumbs and spills.

- Wear a watch or carry a timer with an alarm. When you park at meters, set the alarm to alert you when it's almost time to feed the meter again. It will help you remember and you'll avoid unnecessary parking tickets.

- Keep a checklist in the side pocket of your car door. List everything you don't want to forget such as:

  ❑ Turn off the lights.

  ❑ Take your keys.

  ❑ Empty the trunk.

  ❑ Remove the removable car radio, cassette, or CD player.

  ❑ Roll-up the windows.

- When you bring your car in for service, if your service person doesn't do it for you, jot down the place, current mileage and type

---

*Time is the only coin you have in life . . . and only you can determine how it will be spent. Be careful lest you let other people spend it for you.*

Carl Sandburg

of service. In addition, take note of the next recommended service date and schedule it on your calendar. Taking care of your car regularly, will prolong its life.

- If you don't want to waste time sitting in traffic, don't drive during rush hour. Leave an hour earlier, stay an hour later.

- Get your car washed at the car wash if you don't have time to do it yourself. If you do choose to do it yourself, bring your walkman and listen to a motivational tape or some high-energy music while doing so. You'll be washing your car, exercising and getting motivated all at the same time!

- Instead of going to a gas station that requires you to go inside and wait in line to pay the attendant, find one nearby that allows you to simply swipe your credit card at the pump and go.

- Start a carpool to work, this way you don't have to be the driver every single day. You can spend the passenger time reading the paper or a book.

- Get your oil changed at a Quick-Lube or Jiffy-Lube. It wastes too much time to do it yourself. For the little bit of money, it's worth it to have one of those places do it for you.

- Pocket organizers that hang on the back of the car seat can hold and organize maps and other pertinent traveling information.

- Keep some favorite audio cassettes or CD's in your vehicle for listening enjoyment without having to constantly switch radio stations.

> *You only live once. But if you work it right, once is enough.*
>
> Joe Lewis

## Traveling by Plane, Train or Bus

- Make sure each piece of luggage has a luggage tag secured on it. It should include your name, address and phone number.

- If your budget allows and you fly frequently, join your airline lounge club. You'll eliminate waiting in lines, plus you can make the time you spend in airports more productive since you can complete work on your computer, make calls and review notes.

- Fly direct whenever possible. Otherwise, you'll be spending most of your time waiting, and dealing with delays.

- If your baggage is small and light, carry it on. Waiting for checked baggage can push you over 30 minutes behind.

- Spend a little more money, save a lot of time. Consider taking an express train or bus, rather than one with frequent stops.

- Travel with the same company each time. They'll have all your information listed on their computer—from previous trips. Future reservations will be a snap.

# Travel Checklist

Make copies of this page and use it as your Travel Checklist or duplicate a similar form on your computer.

Simply add in any travel items not already listed. Then, check off each item as you pack it in your suitcase. Bring this list on your trip with you, so you remember to pack everything back up for home.

## Documents

- ___ Airline/Train/Bus/Boat Tickets
- ___ Driver's License
- ___ Emergency Information and Phone Numbers
- ___ Health Documentation
- ___ Insurance Cards
- ___ Passport and Passport Copies/Travel Visa

## Essentials

- ___ Baggage Locks and Keys
- ___ Batteries
- ___ Binoculars
- ___ Briefcase
- ___ Camera, Film and Camera Supplies
- ___ Credit Cards
- ___ Guidebooks
- ___ Hair Dryer
- ___ Keys
- ___ Maps (Local/State/Country)
- ___ Mini-Sewing Kit
- ___ Money
- ___ Purse/Wallet
- ___ Telephone Calling Cards
- ___ Travel Iron
- ___ Traveler's Checks
- ___ Umbrella
- ___ Watch

## Eye Products

- ___ Contact Lenses and Supplies
- ___ Eye Drops
- ___ Reading Glasses
- ___ Sunglasses

## Toiletries

- ___ Brush/Comb
- ___ Deodorant
- ___ Hairspray
- ___ Make up/Make up Remover
- ___ Razor
- ___ Toothbrush
- ___ Toothpaste
- ___ Shaving Cream

- ___ Soap
- ___ Shampoo/Conditioner
- ___ Q-Tips/Cotton Balls

## Outerwear

- ___ Gloves/Mittens/Hat
- ___ Jacket/Coat/Rain Jacket
- ___ Sweater/Sweatshirt/Sweatpants

## Footwear

- ___ Boots
- ___ Sandals
- ___ Shoes/Dress and Casual
- ___ Slippers
- ___ Sneakers
- ___ Socks and Hosiery/Dress and Casual

## Clothing

- ___ Belt/Tie/Other Accessories/Jewelry
- ___ Dress and Casual Pants/Skirts/Tops/Shorts
- ___ Sleepwear/Robe
- ___ Suits/Dresses/Blazers
- ___ Swimsuit/Towel
- ___ Underwear

## Medical/First-Aid

- ___ Antacid
- ___ Aspirin or Other Pain Reliever
- ___ Chapstick
- ___ Insect Repellant
- ___ Insect Bite Salve/Anti-Itch Cream
- ___ Moisturizer
- ___ Nasal Spray
- ___ Prescription Medications
- ___ Suntan Lotion
- ___ Vitamins

## Other

- ___ _____
- ___ _____
- ___ _____
- ___ _____

# Basic Vehicle Maintenance Checklist

Make copies of this page and use it as your Basic Vehicle Maintenance Checklist or duplicate a similar form on your computer. Simply add in any maintenance items not already listed. Then, as maintenance items are done for your vehicle, simply indicate the service date, current mileage and type of service performed.

Lubrication
- Engine Oil Filter
- Engine Oil Change
- Transmission Fluid Change
- Differential/Transaxle Lubricant Change
- Chassis Lubrication
- Fluid Levels Check
- Wheel Bearings (Clean, Repack, Adjust)

Tires
- Check Tire Condition
- Check Spare Tire Condition
- Air Pressure/Tread Depth
- Rotate
- Wheel Balance
- Vehicle Alignment

Engine
- Performance Analysis (Tune-up)
- Spark Plugs
- Air Filter/Fuel Filter
- PCV Filter
- Crankcase Filter
- Canister Filter
- Emission Control System
- Exhaust Analysis

Brakes
- Inspect Brake System
- Brake Fluid Level/Condition
- Flush/Bleed/Adjust Brake System

Cooling System
- Level/Condition
- Antifreeze Protection
- Pressure Test
- Radiator Cap
- Hoses/Clamps/Thermostat
- Power Flush
- Heater Operation

Drive Belts
- Fan and Accessory Belts
- Camshaft/Timing Belt
- Belt/Tension Adjustment

Battery
- Electrolyte Level
- Condition
- Connections/Cable
- Battery Protection Treatment

Air Conditioner
- Performance Test
- Discharge/Evaluate/Recharge
- A/C Filter - Drier
- Leak Test

Steering/Suspension/Exhaust
- Inspect

Lighting/Horn
- Lamps/Bulbs
- Aim Head Lamps
- Brake Lights
- Signal Lights
- Horn Operation

Windshield
- Washer Level/Operation
- Wiper Blades
- Glass

State Inspection
- Safety
- Exhaust Emissions
- Vehicle Registration

| Date | Mileage | Maintenance Completed |
|------|---------|-----------------------|
| _____ | _____ | _____ |
| _____ | _____ | _____ |
| _____ | _____ | _____ |
| _____ | _____ | _____ |
| _____ | _____ | _____ |
| _____ | _____ | _____ |
| _____ | _____ | _____ |
| _____ | _____ | _____ |
| _____ | _____ | _____ |
| _____ | _____ | _____ |
| _____ | _____ | _____ |
| _____ | _____ | _____ |
| _____ | _____ | _____ |
| _____ | _____ | _____ |
| _____ | _____ | _____ |
| _____ | _____ | _____ |

# Chapter 46

❖❖❖❖❖❖❖❖❖❖❖❖❖❖❖❖

# Communication

*Happiness is a
journey;
not a destination.*

Anonymous

E ffective communication, verbal or written, is essential in our business and personal lives. It is the key to both giving and obtaining important information and essential details.

• Express yourself specifically. Suppose that you wish to meet with one of your business associates to discuss a pending deal, but you just tell him that you want to meet for lunch. Since your associate isn't aware that you wish to discuss something of a confidential nature, he decides to bring along a few of his business friends. Once you arrive at the restaurant, you soon realize that because you didn't communicate your intentions to your associate, you now are wasting your time at a meeting that does not address your original goal. Plus, you now have to schedule another meeting!

• Speed up your communication efforts by preparing pre-printed versions of your answers to the most common questions. Anything that you write or say more than once can be effectively duplicated. You can use these for your employees, customers and associates.

• Communicate exactly what you expect, or deal with the consequences of getting exactly what you *didn't* want.

• Create and print out directions to your home and/or business, coming from north, south, east and west. Leave these instructions right by your telephone to give to anyone visiting. Also, make a few copies and keep in a file, ready to send to anyone who needs it.

• Communicate via e-mail whenever possible. You won't waste time on the telephone or writing and formatting a formal letter.

• Have a job for someone to do? Give them your verbal *and* written instructions. Then, have them repeat the vital details back to you. This is a great way of clearing up any confusion and making sure the person understood what you wanted.

• Instead of telling employees what to do and leaving the completion of those tasks to their memories, you are sure to get what you need without question with detailed checklists describing exactly what you want them to do. As they complete each step, they simply check it off on the list. Big companies all do it this way. Imagine NASA, airlines or hospitals running smoothly without checklists!

• Come up with standard form letters that answer common questions.

When a question comes up, simply make a copy of your standard answer letter and send it on its way. No extra work!

- Writing a formal letter may not be necessary to communicate your point. A simple phone call may be all it takes.

- If you're training someone how to use a particular piece of equipment, such as the copy machine, follow this plan of action:

  ✓ Tell them how to do it.

  ✓ Show them how to do it.

  ✓ Ask them to tell it and show it to you.

  Don't just ask him if he understands. He may say "yes," but how will you really know if he truly understood it? After all, something you said could have been miscommunicated or misunderstood. Remember the old saying, *"Tell me and I'll forget. Show me and I might remember. Involve me and I'll learn."*

- Don't expect to communicate through a company newsletter or a memo and assume everybody will be up-to-date. Unfortunately, it doesn't work that way. You have to follow-up with people to make sure they read and understood new policies and so on.

- Create department and company layout maps so new employees won't have to keep asking where things are.

- Have employees keep a 3-ring binder containing answers to their most frequently asked questions, such as "How do I change the copy machine toner?" or "How do I program my telephone?"

- Storyboarding is a great way to communicate and plan when a team is responsible for achieving something. It keeps everyone involved, is an excellent visual, and will save an enormous amount of time.

  [1] Give everyone a thick felt tip marker and index cards.

  [2] Post the problem, project and outcome you are planning for.

  [3] Ask each person to write a one to five word description, giving their ideas on their cards.

  [4] Give them a time limit. Collect and post the cards on the wall.

  [5] Group the cards into categories and discard duplicates.

  [6] Create category headings and, with input from the team, arrange the ideas into a workable plan.

  [7] Assign responsibilities.

  [8] Transfer the plan to paper—or take a photograph of it—and distribute copies to everyone to implement.

  [9] Follow up, meet with your team regularly, and adjust whenever necessary.

*We only hear 25% initially.*

*Of that, we forget 50% within the first hour.*

*Most of that is forgotten within one month.*

*The result . . . We remember less than 5% of verbal communication.*

*Write it down.*

Hermann Ebbinghaus

*By trying to be
everywhere at once
I am nowhere.*

*By trying to be
everyone to too
many I am no one.*

Natasha Josefowitz

## Chapter 47

# Delegation

*I*t's just easier to do it myself. If I only had a dollar for every time I've heard those words. I know many people think it's easier to just do everything themselves. Unfortunately, you can't do everything yourself and give everything 100%. When you're trying to achieve something important, you must concentrate on that vital goal and let go a bit when it comes to other less important things.

- Train your staff if you're fortunate enough to have one and delegate to them. Don't try to do it all yourself. If you have employees, get them to help you.

- If you don't have a staff, there are plenty of companies and individuals that you may be able to outsource to.

- Delegation does not mean that you take something that you absolutely hate to do, dump it on someone else's shoulders and rid yourself of all responsibility. It simply means that you give someone else a task that you don't have time to do, you train the person how to do it and you follow up to ensure it is being done correctly.

- Delegation is a great way to train someone how to complete a particular task or project. Next time a similar job comes along, you'll have someone trained and experienced enough to handle it for you independently with little direction needed.

- Never give a person a task that you're unfamiliar with. Always start by formulating the big picture first, then by making a list of the things that need to be done.

- Select the appropriate person to whom the assignment will be given. Ensure that person has the time, tools and the skill to do what you need done correctly and in a timely manner.

- Make sure the person is clear on the aspects of the assignment, including desired results, time frames and how you'll be tracking their progress. Encourage questions now and in the future.

- Set realistic deadlines. Ask people to complete things a few days before you really need them. This cushion will allow for unexpected last minute problems.

- Ask for feedback to ensure the person understands the assignment and is able to complete it by the deadline.

- Give support and direction throughout the projects as needed, but don't fall into the trap of *doing the work.*

- Answer any questions in a timely manner so the person can complete what they have to do in the timeframe that you expect.

- Remind others when deadlines are coming up. You're not being a pest. You just want to ensure the deadline is met.

- It's vital to keep track of what you're delegating, to whom and when you need it done. Keep a list and check it regularly. When an item is complete, cross it off your list.

- Regularly review and evaluate results. Let everyone know how often you will be doing so.

- When the project has been completed, don't forget to praise the person for a job well done.

- A small gift or handwritten note goes a long way in showing your appreciation. Plus, you'll motivate people to want to do more! Try giving an extra day off from work, a gift certificate for a free lunch or something else you know this person would really enjoy.

- Outsource for business and personal reasons. You can outsource printing, telephone answering, direct mailings and more for your business and painting, decorating, lawn care and more for your home. Specialists can always accomplish more in less time, since they have the knowledge, skill, equipment and experience.

- When outsourcing, give complete and specific instructions. Put them in writing. Ensure the person understands you by having them explain what needs to be done back to you, especially if this is going to be an expensive project.

- Sometimes, if the project isn't too intense, you can delegate to a high school or college student. This is very cost effective for time consuming projects such as those that require heavy data entry. Call your local university and ask if you could post a project opportunity on their bulletin board.

- Advertise a project opportunity in your community or church bulletin. Instead of hiring someone permanently, you can hire someone temporarily to get the pending project completed.

- Most people think of delegation as giving something to someone else to do. But you could also delegate to your computer or your answering machine. Instead of responding to requests for information on your website, delegate this responsibility to an auto responder. Rather than picking up every telephone call that comes in, delegate this responsibility to your answering machine or voice mail.

*Help!*
*I need somebody.*

The Beatles

## Chapter 48

# Meetings

**M**eetings that have specific objectives and effective leaders running them usually can get a ton of projects started and completed. However, meetings that are unplanned, unscheduled, lacking goals, lacking deadlines and/or run by committees are generally very ineffective. Get organized, and make every meeting you host or attend worth your while.

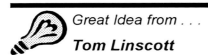

### Great Idea from . . .
### Tom Linscott

*We used to hold weekly management meetings that lasted hours and never accomplished anything. There weren't any clearly defined goals or responsibilities.*

*Our new system is to use an "Action Agenda." It includes the overall projects, individual project tasks, deadlines and the people responsible for completing each task.*

*At each meeting, we simply use the Action Agenda to review the status of our projects and what each person has done so far.*

*With this Action Agenda, we always keep on track, our meetings are shorter and we're accomplishing more than ever!*

Tom Linscott, Wauwatosa, WI

Tom is the co-owner of Gilles Frozen Custard (oldest custard stand in Milwaukee - in business for over 60 years). He is the proud Dad of William and Catherine.

## Leading a Meeting

• If attendees don't know each other, prepare nametags for each of them. On the day of the meeting, arrange them alphabetically outside the meeting room for attendees to pick up and use.

• Be prepared for your meetings. Lack of preparation will waste everyone's time.

• Be on time. You should arrive at meetings you're holding well ahead of time, anywhere from 15 minutes to an hour, depending on how much equipment you have to set up and test.

• If you hold meetings, avoid Monday mornings. People need time to start their week and tie up any loose ends from the previous week.

• Avoid Friday meetings. You can't stop people from dreaming about the weekend. Plus an immense amount of information will be forgotten by the time everyone is back to work on them.

• Always prepare written agendas for your meetings and distribute them to the attendees a minimum of one to two days before the meeting. Include the meeting start and end time to keep the meeting on schedule.

• Set time limits for each topic. Indicate this on the agenda.

• Don't wait for latecomers. Start without them, unless of course, they're your supervisors or clients.

• To make sure everyone gets to your meetings on time, have the last person to arrive take the minutes. People generally hate to do this and will run to the meeting to ensure they're not the last one there.

- Set timers in meetings to keep on track. Kitchen timers work very well. Set the timer for 20 minutes, or the amount of time needed to take care of the first topic. When the alarm goes off, it is time to move on to the next topic. Hopefully, you wrapped up your goals for the initial topic, but if not, write down where you left off so that you can pick up on it at the end of the meeting if you have time, or at the next meeting.

- Meeting Minutes are notes taken on what was discussed and what decisions were made. Take notes at meetings you attend. However, if you're leading the meeting, delegate this responsibility to someone else. There's no way that you can take notes and speak to a group at the same time and not miss something.

- If you like holding meetings at restaurants, but feel you are spending too much time at luncheon meetings, consider late afternoon coffee meetings instead. You'll have a nice break to briefly escape the phones and interruptions, without spending too much time out of the office. Another plus is that the restaurant will be empty, making it a good forum to talk business.

## Attending a Meeting

- Be prepared for your meetings. Lack of preparation eats up more time than you can imagine.

- If you feel that your presence is not necessary at a particular meeting, and you can get out of it, a lot of time will be saved and your day will be more productive.

- Jot down any necessary notes that concern you or people you're responsible for. Don't try to eliminate the notes and remember everything that was discussed. You're bound to forget something.

- When you're going to a meeting outside the office, always reconfirm the time and place *before* you leave. You'll save time and embarrassment, if for some reason the meeting was cancelled and nobody was able to reach you.

- If you have plans to meet with someone from out of town, ask them where they're staying. Request the phone number and name of the hotel. Jot the information into your planner so that you can contact them in case of cancellation, change of plans or simply to confirm.

- If you're running late for a meeting, call and inform the necessary people. Their time is valuable too.

- Always suggest that a meeting leader be appointed to keep the meeting on track. Without a leader at a meeting, it is nearly impossible to achieve anything.

*In order to see one's own direction, one must simplify the mechanics of ordinary, everyday life.*

Plato

*A man who wears
two watches,
never knows the
correct time.*

Chinese Proverb

# Chapter 49

# Appointments

An appointment is a scheduled time to be somewhere or to meet someone at a specific, pre-designated time. Unfortunately, in the real world, appointments don't always work out as we'd like them to. Even if we're always there on time, that doesn't mean we'll totally escape some time in a waiting room.

There are some things you can do to schedule appointments more effectively. In addition, if you are caught waiting, make the very most of the extra few minutes.

- Avoid scheduling appointments when the entire world is scheduling them. Avoid going to the post office, bank or restaurant during the typical lunch hour. If your doctor is usually extremely busy from 11:00AM-1:00PM, ask for an appointment later in the afternoon.

- When you visit your doctor or dentist, schedule your next appointment on the spot. This way, you won't have to waste time later and you won't forget to make your necessary appointments.

- Don't play the waiting game. Try your best to book the first appointment in the morning or the first one after lunch. That way, it's unlikely that anyone will be ahead of you.

- If you have no choice except to wait, do another errand within walking distance. If you have no errands to run, use the time productively by writing up a list of items you must do tomorrow or by reading that pending report or article.

- If you can, bring your office to your appointment. This way, while you're waiting you can work. Bring your laptop computer and cellular phone along and be productive.

- Never go to an appointment without confirming first. There is always a chance that the party you're supposed to meet has forgotten about the scheduled date.

- An appointment is simply a mutual agreement to meet with someone at a specific time. Next time you can't find time to take a walk, exercise, read something of interest or do something else nice for yourself, schedule an appointment with yourself and write it on your calendar. When the time comes, keep the appointment, just as you would any other. You are too important to put yourself and the things you love to do on the backburner.

## Chapter 50

## Interruptions

E*xcuse me. Can I waste your time for a minute?* That's basically what most interruptions boil down to. Think about it. The last time someone interrupted you, was the building on fire or was some other emergency happening? Probably not.

Interruptions, people and other, soak up our time like a sponge. They bar us from completing our projects and cause missed deadlines.

Avoid interruptions at all costs.

- Do you allow people to interrupt you because you're concerned about offending them? Use these kind phrases and most people will get the message that you're busy, without being insulted:

    ✓ *Sorry, I'm not able to talk to you right now. Can I get back to you at noon?*

    ✓ *I'm on my way out the door. May I call you back tomorrow at ten, or would the afternoon be better for you?*

    ✓ *It's been great talking, but right now I need to complete a project. Let's pick up on this subject tomorrow or next week.*

- If your business is one that requires frequent co-worker interaction, schedule specific time periods in your day for those meetings. For example, let everyone know that you're only available for one-on-one conversation between 2:00 and 4:00.

- Encourage people to use e-mail in the office, so you can answer questions and share ideas when it's convenient, rather than constantly being interrupted.

- Keep a sign on your desk, with the following questions, as a visual reminder to help you eliminate interruptions.

    ✓ Does this interruption really need to be handled immediately?
    ✓ Can this interruption be deterred until a later time?
    ✓ Can this interruption be diverted to someone else?

- When interrupted, jot down a small note to remind yourself where you left off. You'll get quickly back on track without wasting time.

- Establish specific time periods when you're available to speak with people. Let your assistant know that you're available only within this designated time period.

*There are people who do not know how to waste their time all by themselves. They are the scourge of active people.*

Louis de Bonald

## *Using Checklists*

A simple, but effective idea for eliminating interruptions is to create detailed checklists for people helping you out. This way, they can work independently, complete all necessary steps without forgetting and reduce the need to interrupt you with questions.

Once, I helped Betty, a client, develop detailed checklists so that her employees could send a fax without having to interrupt her.

The checklists were very simple to create and were formatted like this one below:

**Sending a Fax**

__  1.  Insert the paper, face-down, into the paper feeder on the fax machine. Make sure it grabs the paper.

__  2.  Press the VOICE button.

__  3.  When you hear the dial tone, dial "1," the area code and the appropriate fax number.

__  4.  When you hear a connection tone, press SEND.

__  5.  When the paper is finished faxing, be sure to take the original with you.

We created over 100 simple checklists for Betty, similar to the one above.

Betty used to be interrupted a hundred times a day. Just by creating and instituting this simple simple, Betty was able to reduce interruptions in her workday by over 60%.

Wow! A simple system, but a huge benefit!

- Avoid eye contact with people passing your office. Face your desk away from the door.

- Visitor chairs encourage people to stop and relax. Temporarily remove the chairs until you have a legitimate appointment.

- Bring your project to a quieter spot where you're less likely to be interrupted, such as an unused office in your company, another room in your home or the public library.

- Write instructions and checklists for your employees to use for common tasks and projects. This will eliminate the possibility of them interrupting you with the same questions being asked again and again.

- Keep your door closed, otherwise you're inviting interruption. Put up a DO NOT DISTURB sign.

- Make a list of the people in your life that have no respect for your time. Then limit the time you spend with them.

- If you're constantly checking the traffic, people or weather out of your window, move your desk or shut the blinds. The window distraction can waste hundreds of minutes.

- Do employees interrupt you with questions all day? That's because you don't have a system in place to handle these recurring inquiries. Create an Employee Policy Manual. Make employee checklists. Designate a few managers. Do everything you can so employees know company policies and can do their jobs independently.

- Although they would never admit it, some people love to be interrupted, because that means they can stop whatever they're doing. Then, they use the interruption as an excuse for not being able to finish their projects or meet their deadlines. Just, food for thought.

- Screen your telephone calls. In other words, let them all go into Voicemail or your answering machine. Finish your project without any interruptions. Then simply return any calls later in the day, during your scheduled telephone hour.

- Turn off your radio—or if you work at home, shut off the television set. You're probably aware that working when your favorite song is on or when the TV talk show host is telling a funny story is not nearly as productive as quiet time.

- If you have a home office, make sure your family—especially your children—understand that just because you're home, that doesn't mean you're not working. Don't give in to them, even though they may look at you with sad, irresistible faces. Send them away until you're finished with what you're working on.

# Chapter 51

# Eliminating Procrastination

We're all guilty of procrastination at one point or another in our lives. You know how it is. That decision we know we have to make, but let it linger on and on in hopes that it will just take care of itself. We procrastinate for a few common reasons:

- ✓ We figure we don't have the time for the action that is necessary.
- ✓ We are concerned that the outcome may hurt someone or be otherwise unfavorable.
- ✓ We don't have enough information to make the decision.
- ✓ We don't have a specific deadline to make the decision by.
- ✓ We don't know how to make a decision.
- ✓ We don't understand why a decision needs to be made, and how to go about deciding.

When we fail to make decisions, we leave everything up to chance. That's like basing our lives on the lottery with a very miniscule chance of it working itself out and a very big chance of an unfortunate turnout.

Take the bull by the horns. Control your destiny.

- Don't spend all your time fretting over trivial decisions, like what brand of paper you should purchase or if you should buy the $9 item instead of the $9.23 item. Give important decisions the attention they deserve and force yourself to make immediate decisions on the rest.

- People use trivial tasks as an excuse for not working on the important stuff. Beware of this time waster. You'll never catch up.

- Procrastination is your enemy. Instead of putting things off completely, do a little bit each day. A little bit done is much better than nothing done.

- Start with the end result in mind. Get yourself a bunch of index cards. On one, write down the end result. On the others, using one card for each thought, write down something that needs to be done to achieve the end result. It doesn't have to be in any particular order just yet. When you can't think of anything else you need to do, begin arranging the cards, putting them in a logical order. You should now be ready to tackle the projects, card by card.

*You shouldn't make someone else's choices.*

*You shouldn't let someone else make yours.*

General Colin Powell

- Narrow down your options. Make a pro and con list. The option that gets the most "pros" and the least "cons" wins!

- Gather the necessary information you need to make a decision. If you're not sure what you need, get someone to help or research it yourself. Once the information is available, the decision may become very obvious.

  • Set a deadline and make your decision by that date. Don't let it drag out too long. The longer you procrastinate, the harder the decision will be.

  • Get a close friend, associate or specialist to help you weigh your options. It's often easier to make a decision when someone is there to help.

  • If your deadline arrives and you still haven't made a decision, flip a coin and go with that choice. Control your destiny.

  • Harry Truman once said, "Whenever I make a bum decision, I just go out and make another decision." In other words, don't let your fear of making a bad decision, stop you from making any decision at all.

- Write what you have to do on an index card. Post it where you can see it often. For instance, if you have a project to work on and can't seem to get started, write a statement on your card that says, "I intend to begin the first part of my project today at 3:00 and work straight through until 4:00. When done, I will reward myself with an hour of guilt-free time at the golf course."

- Announce your intention publicly. Tell your friends, spouse, roommates, parents or children. Make it known; make the world your support group. Telling the world of your intention is an excellent technique to ensure its completion.

- Take it one small step at a time. Don't keep thinking, "What is the next step on my list?" Rather, think, "I'll concentrate on this one step for right now."

- Optimize your chances for success. Don't say, I'll get to it later. Instead say, "I'm going to lock myself in my office from 2:00 until 4:00 today and work exclusively on Parts A and B of this project."

- When you notice yourself continually putting a task on the back-burner, re-examine the purpose for doing it at all. If you really don't intend to do something, stop telling yourself that you will. Be honest with yourself and drop it. You then don't have to carry around the baggage of an undone task.

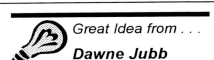
*Great Idea from . . .*
**Dawne Jubb**

*My motto is, "Do it when you have to do it, and don't put it off." You'll get more done than you ever dreamed possible.*

Dawne Jubb, St. Francis, WI

Proud mother of Justen who is a United States Marine.

# Chapter 52

# Effective Reading

L iving in the Information Age has increased the number of publications available to a preposterously high number. We really have to be choosy about what we read, because there's just not enough time in our lives for covering everything.

For those publications that we do wish to read, getting organized is a major benefit. Doing so will help us make time to read the publications we choose and in addition, help us to get through that reading material as quickly as possible.

- When reading newspapers and magazines, read with a highlighter. When you find something that you could use—such as a statistic or something you wish to reference in the future—simply highlight the appropriate area. Then, when you're done reading the publication, clip out the article, write the name and issue on the back so you have it for reference and file it in an appropriate folder.

- Instead of reading word for word, quickly skim through publications, scanning each page. Highlight or circle all headlines that are of interest to you. This should only take a few minutes. Then, go back and read only those marked articles.

- If you don't have time right now to read those articles that you highlighted, you may want to tear out the pages and schedule a time to read them later on. This way, you don't have to go through the entire publication again to determine what it was that you wanted to read. Plus, you won't be saving unnecessary newspaper and magazine clutter.

- When reading a book, use an index card book mark to remember sections that you'd like to reference later or share with someone else. On your index card, write down the page number, the area of the page (T=Top, M=Middle, B=Bottom) and 1-3 words to help you remember what it was that interested you. It's a waste of time to look through the entire book again to find something. Leave that card in the book, or in a card file box for easy access later.

- If you have an enormous volume of information to keep up with, you may want to consider taking a speed reading class. Some local universities offer these classes. Use the phone book and/or the web to locate classes in your area. Or you can choose to do it on your own, either by buying a book or borrowing one from your library.

*(When asked late in life why he was studying geometry)*

**If I should not be learning now, when should I be?**

Lacydes

- Schedule a specific time to read every day—15-30 minutes minimum—and indicate this appointment on your calendar. Keep that appointment with yourself. In doing this, reading will soon become part of your daily routine and you'll keep current with the never-ending stream of information that flows through your office.

- Listen to books on audio tape. It will keep you up to date, while allowing versatility. You can listen while in the car, exercising, taking a break in the office or lying on the beach.

- When spending your day out of the office, put all or some of your day's reading into a Traveling Reading Folder. Then, whenever you have the opportunity during the day, your reading material will be easily accessible. Some opportune times to read are while waiting in someone's office for an appointment, riding on the train or bus and waiting in long lines.

- Prioritize reading material. Assign a code to everything you're determined to read:

  ❖ A=High Priority: It's imperative that I read this immediately or within the week.

  ❖ B=Medium Priority: I have or want to read this, although I have a few weeks or a month to do so.

  ❖ C=Low Priority: I don't have to read this, although it may be interesting if I have time.

- Read the TV Guide with two highlighters. Highlight your first choices with a yellow highlighter and your second choices with a green one. Later, you can skim the guide in seconds and choose your programming at a glance.

- Here's a system for those articles you wish to save for future reference. Categorize your articles into a few different subjects and make a labeled folder for each category (Marketing, Employees, etc.) Then, assign a subject code, plus a sequential number, to each article (eg. MK1=Marketing Article 1.) Jot that code in the top, right corner of the article and place it in the proper, categorized file folder. Then keep a computer list of the article name and subject/numerical code of each article for quick reference later. Example:

**Marketing File Folder**
6 Ideas for an Effective Direct Mail Campaign....................MK1
How Mr. Rich Marketed His Business.............................MK2
Marketing on the Web......................................MK3

**Employee File Folder**
Motivating Employees for High Performance......................EM1
Establishing Employee Goals...............................EM2

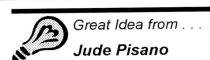

*Great Idea from . . .*
**Jude Pisano**

*When reading a newspaper or book, keep a dictionary nearby. You'll be able to look up an unfamiliar word in a jiffy.*

Jude Pisano, North Bergen, NJ

Jude is my sister. She is a registered nurse in St. Francis Hospital. Her cat's name is Sophie.

## Chapter 53

# Eliminating Reading Clutter

**B**ooks. Magazines. Newspapers. Articles. Periodicals. Pamphlets. Brochures. Legal Documents. Policies. Notes. Letters. Memos. E-mail. I'll stop now, but this list could go on and on. There are a million things to read, but only 24 hours in a day. To eliminate clutter—and a fire hazard—get your reading materials organized. Keep only what you're really going to benefit from. Discard the rest.

- Since newspapers contain current events, those that are more than a day or two old generally contain old news. Throw them out.

- Create a "To Read" file or tray to store all of your reading material. It's much easier to determine how much you have to read, when it's stored in one location, instead of all over your office.

- Use a Magazine Box to store magazines and catalogs you wish to keep. Don't let it get out of hand though. Exchange old ones with new ones and throw the old ones out.

- If your "To Read" pile is beginning to look like a mountain, then you're not dedicating enough time to read everything you want to. You may be trying to bite off more than you can chew. Keep this in mind when you're placing articles in your "To Read" file or tray and you'll avoid unnecessary reading clutter.

- Do you have books that you've already read, but didn't enjoy, and will never look at again? You may consider passing them on to your local library or book reseller.

- Discard publications and memos that are outdated. Skim through them if you need to. Clip and file only those items that are absolutely necessary.

- If you love books and must have your own personal copies of them, this tip is not for you. But, if you're an avid reader, you'll save space and money by just borrowing your books from the library.

- Print labels that say "This book belongs to _____". When you lend a book to someone, he or she won't forget who they borrowed it from. Keep a list of books you loan and dates you expect them back so you can contact the borrower if necessary. (*Here's another idea:* Place a 3" x 5" card in the book with the words, "Please return this book to _____ (your name) by _____ (date.)"

*The force is within you. Force yourself.*

Harrison Ford

- Certain publications that cross your desk are time sensitive.
    - ✓ Letters or Memos ............ Discard if no longer current.
    - ✓ Daily Newspapers ............ Discard if older than 1 week.
    - ✓ Weekly Magazines ........... Discard if older than 1 month.
    - ✓ Monthly Magazines .......... Discard if older than 3 months.

- If you have a substantial amount of reading to keep up with, keep two deep trays, labeled "To Read":
    - ✓ **TRAY 1: A & B Priorities:** Schedule a specific date and time on your calendar for your A and B reading priorities.
        - ❖ A=High Priority: It's imperative that I read this immediately or within the week. (Keep in a Red folder in the tray.)
        - ❖ B=Medium Priority: I have or want to read this, although I have a few weeks or a month to do so.
    - ✓ **TRAY 2: C Priorities:** Your C priorities can be read in your spare time, but force yourself to have no more than 5 items in this tray at the same time. Force yourself to make a trade. Take something out of your tray and throw it away, before replacing it with the new item.
        - ❖ C=Low Priority: I don't have to read this, although it may be interesting if I have time.

- Are you a subscription junkie? Ask yourself . . .
    - ✓ How long have I been reading this publication?
    - ✓ How often do I do anything more than glance at it?
    - ✓ What would I miss if I stopped receiving it?

    As you ask yourself these questions, keep the essential publications. Cancel your subscriptions to the rest.

- If you order from mail-order catalogs and you like to keep them around for a little while, keep them in a magazine holder. Many office supplies stores have inexpensive, but sturdy, cardboard ones. Keep catalogs in your holder on a shelf. Make sure when the most current catalog arrives, you replace the old one with the new one.

- Arrange your books on bookshelves in alphabetical order by genre and title. Example:

    | | |
    |---|---|
    | Biographies | A, B, C, D, etc. |
    | Mysteries | A, B, C, D, etc. |
    | Romance | A, B, C, D, etc. |

- Store bookmarks in a basket near the common reading area. When a family member is looking for one, they'll know where to find it.

*Dost thou love life? Then do not squander time; for that's the stuff life is made of.*

Benjamin Franklin

## Chapter 54

❖❖❖❖❖❖❖❖❖❖❖❖❖❖❖❖❖

# Purchases and Bill Paying

I love getting mail. Well, not all mail. Bills are not my favorite by a long shot. In fact, my husband always laughs because I get to open all the fun stuff and he gets to open all the bills.

Everybody wants our money. Since we need food, shelter, water, clothing, transportation and microwave ovens to survive, we readily empty our hard earned money into someone else's cash register.

## Bill Paying

- Decide on a dedicated place to collect, review and pay your incoming bills. Designate that place your permanent bill paying area.

- Create a workable bill payment and money management system. You can do this with a calculator, pen and paper; or you can go the more sophisticated route by using one of the many money management, computer software programs available, such as Quicken™.

- If you do decide to use money management software, you can set it up to automatically remind you of upcoming payments and invoices due. It can also automatically print out your checks, keep track of your expenses and provide you with detailed reports of your transaction history

- Don't lose track of the checks you write or you'll never know how much is in your account. Always enter the check information into the check register, before tearing out the check.

- Balance your checkbook when your bank statement arrives. This will help correct any mistakes made by you or your bank.

- After paying a bill, mark it PAID with the date. Purchase a stamp/inkpad set that allows you to change the date and mark your paid bills effortlessly.

- Keep essential supplies and tools, pertinent to bill paying, in close reach. This may include your computer, a calculator, your checkbook, pens, envelopes, a letter opener, self-stick return address labels and postage stamps.

- Set up a monthly budget and schedule. Set time aside at least twice

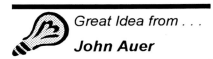

### Great Idea from . . .

### John Auer

*Before you turn over the page in your checkbook, double check your addition and subtraction on that page. This way you won't be carrying arithmetic errors on for pages and pages.*

Johnny A, Brown Deer, WI

John is a retired computer guy. He is grandpa to Kelsey, Briana and Matthew.

a month to pay your bills (e.g. the 8th and 22nd of each month.)

- You can pay some companies without ever writing them a check. Some companies can automatically deduct your payments from your checking account each month if you like.

## Credit Cards

- Consolidate whenever you can. Sometimes it's unnecessary to have 20 different bank accounts or 10 different credit cards. Consolidation can give you more control over your finances, plus it greatly reduces the time it takes to pay everything. Most businesses take Visa, MasterCard and/or American Express. Fewer cards allow better control, thus saving you time and money.

- If you absolutely must have a number of credit cards, register them with a company that will cancel them with one phone call if they're stolen or lost.

- Make a list of your credit card numbers—name of the card, card number, expiration date and any listed phone numbers. Keep this list in a safe, inconspicuous area, so that it can be retrieved in an instant in the unfortunate event of a loss.

- Don't carry all of your credit cards everywhere you go. Keep a few major ones in your wallet—Visa, MasterCard, American Express, Discover—and leave the rest at home. If you need to go to a particular store, bring only that store's credit card.

## Money Management

- The American Bankers Association confirms that the single largest reason people overdraw their checking accounts is math errors. It's very easy to make a mistake in math calculation when doing it manually or even with a calculator. Money management software can be an effective, time saving tool that can eliminate many, if not all, math calculation errors.

- It can initially take a few hours to set up money management software, but if it's quality software, such as Quicken™, once it's set up it can make your money management and bill paying a breeze.

- Time is no longer wasted writing out your checks. Many of these software packages have built-in memorization, which allows them to remember recurring payments, addresses, account numbers, etc. with just a few keystrokes. Your account can be balanced and your checks can be printed in minutes.

*Time as he grows old teaches all things.*

Aeschylus

- If you have a modem, you may be able to pay many of your bills online, without leaving your office or home. In addition, companies such as American Express, allow you to view your balances, review recent charges and download transactions—all in minutes.

- You can program your software to automatically remind you of upcoming payments and invoices due. It can also automatically print out your checks, keep track of your expenses and provide you with detailed reports of your transaction history.

- The prices of these software packages are not out of reach for the average individual or business. Some can be purchased for around $100. The more sophisticated programs may cost a little more.

- Do some research before purchasing money management software. Find out how each of the programs can help you and how they compare with each other. While some of the more expensive programs offer a multitude of features, you may not really need all of the extra bells and whistles.

- Be sure to always back-up your money management computer files—keep an extra copy—on floppy, CD-rom or zip drives. Better to be safe than sorry.

## Purchases

- Consider not only the cost of the item itself, but also all related costs. Take the time to think out your purchase, on paper. For example, if you're buying an expensive car, determine if you can afford future repairs, fuel costs, insurance and so on.

- Before you make your next purchase—furniture, appliance, electronics—be certain that you'll really use it. Will it save you time? Will it help you reach your goals? Will it make you happy? Beware of impulse buys.

- Write down what you're looking for in the product/service—size, benefits, features, price. Then, give your list to sales clerks and let them show you what products/services meet your needs.

- Before you purchase something just because it's on sale, think again. If it's on sale, but you don't need it, it's not a bargain.

- Use a comparison chart when you're planning on buying an expensive item. A simple grid comparing features and benefits will help you make the right decision.

- The internet is a wonderful resource for getting details on a variety of products and options. Read reviews on specific company websites and independent opinion message boards.

*Many people take no care of their money till they come nearly to the end of it, and others do just the same thing with their time.*

Goethe

*The only difference between a good day and a bad day is your attitude.*

Dennis S. Brown

# Chapter 55

❖ ❖ ❖ ❖ ❖ ❖ ❖ ❖ ❖ ❖ ❖ ❖ ❖ ❖ ❖ ❖

# Accounting and Taxes

April 15. Need I say more? I find it funny to watch the evening news on this infamous day when tax returns must be post-marked by midnight. There are always thousands of people waiting in lines at the Post Offices around the country desperately trying to mail their tax return before the pending deadline.

- You may not want to hear this, especially if you don't usually expect refunds, but it would save time and stress if you take care of your tax preparation and mailing no later than a week before April 15. In addition, there are a few simple things you can do to help yourself prepare and to avoid your accountant's despair as 10 boxes stuffed with receipts are literally dumped onto his or her desk.

- Keep all of your day-to-day receipts in categorized envelopes. This way, you will be able to quickly and easily match up charges with your credit card statements, find receipts for returns you may need to make and have everything in one area to take to your accountant for tax preparation.

- Each year, set up categorized envelopes for receipts from items and services you purchased. Some of these categories are: Office Supplies, Postage, Printing, Automotive, Business Meals, Entertainment, Travel, Education, etc. Then, whenever you make a purchase, simply slip the receipt into its appropriate categorized envelope. All the information will be at your fingertips for the entire year. At the end of the year, simply file all of the categorized envelopes away and start new envelopes with the same categories again for the new year.

- As you receive W-2's, bank interest statements and other documents related to your taxes, immediately place them in labeled envelopes so they're ready to bring to the accountant or for you to prepare your taxes.

- You may be entitled to a sizable tax write-off for items you donate to charity. A service called, Client Valuation Services, Inc. offers an inexpensive booklet listing hundreds of clothing and household items, plus the amount you can deduct for each. To order, call 800-875-5927 or visit their website: http://www.taxsave.com

- Organize your savings efforts. Deduct a fixed amount from each paycheck and immediately deposit it in the bank.

## Chapter 56

# Computer

In 1943, Tom Watson, founder of IBM, said, "I think there is a world market for maybe five large computers." Well, his idea back then was slightly off base. Obviously, computers have become a normal part of everyday life. If you don't have a computer for your home and business, you're a big step behind. They store tons of information and can save you hours of precious time.

- Don't type out or write names/addresses on envelopes to the same people day after day. Use your computer to preprint batches of labels ahead of time. Keep them stored alphabetically in a file near the area that you do your mailing.

- If your computer has a tower type CPU, you will save desk space by putting the tower on the floor. Just be careful that the unit is securely positioned and that it's properly grounded. Your computer manufacturer may even be able to sell you appropriate stands.

- Use a clip-on light in your computer center. It takes up little space, can be easily moved and provides just the right amount of lighting.

- Instead of leaving your keyboard on your computer desk, install an under-the-desk sliding drawer/shelf. It will neatly hold your keyboard, while allowing you the extra space.

- Use computer short-cut keys for functions you use frequently. The less keystrokes you have to use, the less time you'll waste. In addition, if you're really advanced, macros are a great function to add to the tasks that you perform in the same manner over and over again.

- When purchasing a computer desk or unit, consider the accessories you're going to need to store, such as CD-roms, manuals and disks. Then, purchase a unit that meets those needs.

- Don't let your computer sit around just gathering dust. If you are not familiar with its uses, take a class, read some books or get a friend to help. It's amazing how much time it can save you.

- An effective, organized printer stand is one that holds your printer, but also holds printer paper and perhaps a drawer for your printer manual and disks.

- Create a word processing file for each directory or folder on your computer. Indicate the name of the file and a couple of words to describe it. Then, next time you're searching for a file, you won't

*The reason the computer can do work faster than a human is that it doesn't have to answer the phone.*

Anonymous

have to open up each one individually. You can just go to your word processing index and search for words that match what you're looking for, using your "find" feature.

- Use disk holders to hold your diskettes and zip drive disks, otherwise they're going to get lost or damaged.

- Keep those disks and CD-roms you use most often near the computer and within easy reach.

- Keep the same type of information on each disk. For instance, all of your sales letters could be on one disk, and all employee information on another. Don't mix information. It's liable to take you hours to find what you need.

- Organize CD-roms and computer disks. Use color-coded labels to label your data. Keep them in dust free holders. The disks you use most often should be in the front and easily accessible. Label disks and CD-roms clearly with the category.

- Don't run the risk of losing everything on your hard-drive, in case of a computer crash or malfunction. Purchase a zip drive, or back up your vital files on disk once a day.

- When working on a long document, save it every 10-15 minutes. This way you won't waste time having to redo *everything* in case of a power loss or malfunction.

- Use a database to send out sales letters, invoices, correspondence and other paperwork to a consistent list of people every week or month. Once you have a database, you can easily:

  ✓ Track who you sent information to.
  ✓ Determine what you sent to them.
  ✓ Find out if they responded to you
  ✓ Determine whose birthday is in a particular month—so that you can send greeting cards, discounts, etc.
  ✓ Print out labels to stick on envelopes or self-mailers

- Either create the database yourself using a software program such as Access™, MS Works™, Act™, or a number of other titles. Or, you can contract with a programmer to put a custom database together for you. You'll be amazed at how a good database can help you save time and money!

- Don't keep disks—software programs or files you've created—that you don't need. Purge any individual files on each disk that are outdated.

- Consider a planner that can be linked to computer calendar software. These allow you to print out your address book or calendar in

---

### Great Idea from . . .
### Marilyn Butz

*When writing e-mails, I like to include messages—promotional and other—to my readers, after my salutation. These are commonly called 'sig lines' (or signature lines). I use at least 40 sig lines, maybe more, including standard responses that I use frequently.*

*So, I send an e-mail to myself, with the appropriate subject, and store it in an e-mail folder.*

*When I want to include a sig in an e-mail, I just go to my folder, and select the appropriate one. I then copy and paste it into my e-mail.*

*This eliminates the need to recall my sig lines by memory, plus helps to keep them in a handy file so that I can retrieve them in an instant, without having to retype.*

Marilyn Butz
bizcardpro

Color price and foil all show, your card was made by bizcardpro!

http://bizcardpro.com
Mailto:mm@bizcardpro.com

a size and format that slips right into your planner.

- Still using out-of-date equipment or old versions of computer programs? Calculate how much time you're wasting by using slow equipment and programs with limited capabilities. While new equipment isn't cheap, it may not be wise to spend your valuable time using slow, unproductive tools.

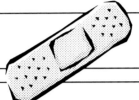

# Organizing Clinic

Question from . . . **Pat Beadle, Jewett, OH**

**Q.** *Is there a way to use my computer to help me remember when to do certain weekly household chores? My husband and I have this computer, and we feel that there has got to be something we could do to make it easier to remember what needs to be done. Maybe some sort of checklist?*

(Pat and John Beadle have 5 children and 5 grandchildren. Both are retired and are now running a tree farm. They're enjoying their faith, family, friends and their dog, Lucky. Pat and John enjoy playing golf.)

**A.** Pat, while you can certainly make some Chore Tables on your computer and print them out, that's probably as far as I'd advise you for using your computer for something like household chores. Since you generally do the same exact tasks from week to week, and month to month, it's not really necessary to keep going back to the computer, except for any minor revisions.

Use a word processor or spreadsheet program to create a Weekly Chore Table, similar to the one below.

Then, simply make copies of your Table. Each week, simply do the chores on your list, crossing off the day/time of each chore as you complete it.

However, since you do have a computer, you can certainly start putting it to good use. Enter common names and addresses into it to have on hand. Then, you can print out labels for holiday cards without having to write them all out each year. Set up a monthly budget and have the computer do the calculations for you. Install money management software and use it as your check writing and tracking system, instead of doing it manually. Install online software, sign up with a provider and surf the web for both educational research and entertainment. Your options are endless.

*Example of a Weekly Chore Table*

| Chores | Mon | Tue | Wed | Thu | Fri | Sat | Sun |
|---|---|---|---|---|---|---|---|
| Dust | 9:00A | — | — | — | — | — | — |
| Vacuum | 10:00A | — | — | — | — | — | — |
| Wash Clothes | — | — | 9:00A | — | — | — | — |
| Dry Clothes | — | — | 10:00A | — | — | — | — |
| Iron | — | — | 11:00A | — | — | — | — |
| Clean Bathroom | — | — | — | 9:00A | — | — | — |
| Empty Garbage | — | 7:00P | — | — | 7:00P | — | — |
| Mow Lawn | — | — | — | — | — | 7:00A | — |

# Chapter 57

# E-mail and Web Surfing

Y ou've got mail! Even after all the time that e-mail has been available, I'm sure you'll agree it's still exciting to notice a message waiting for you in your e-mail in-box. Between e-mail and the internet, I don't know how we ever got along without them.

## E-mail

- Use your online service's virtual address book, if you have one, to store frequently used e-mail addresses and who they belong to. They'll be on hand when you need to e-mail someone.

- If your online service doesn't come equipped with a virtual address book, create a computer or paper list of common e-mail addresses and who they belong to.

- Just like paper, e-mail can soon turn into clutter. Delete messages as soon as you handle the action necessary or as soon as it is no longer useful.

- For those e-mail messages you wish to keep, sort e-mail within the program by topic or person.

- If your online service is equipped with a Personal Filing Cabinet, you can store important e-mails right within the online software program.

- Don't forward tons of jokes and other such things to friends and associates. An occasional joke is fine, but a volume of them is a waste of time; time that could be much better spent.

- If you have an e-mail message that you'd like to send to a number of different people, don't send them individually. Send them all together. Most online services offer carbon copy options or group options.

- Always put *specific* subject headings in your e-mail messages. With the volume of e-mail the average person receives these days, your subject must really stand out and be specific to get noticed ahead of all the other e-mails.

- Be careful of opening files that have been attached to e-mails, unless you're absolutely sure there isn't a virus attached. Take every precaution you can, otherwise, you're going to spend a lot of time

---

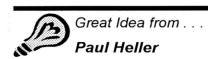

*Great Idea from . . .*
*Paul Heller*

*When you receive a myriad of e-mail messages to rummage through, prioritize them by source and subject, in order not to waste valuable time.*

*Discard insignificant e-mail messages like you would junk mail. You can probably delete a whole bunch without ever opening them.*

Paul Heller
Research Director, MGM Networks

trying to recover lost files on your computer. Use virus protection software.

- Don't spend too much time changing e-mail font styles, sizes, colors, background colors, etc. It's highly likely that your recipient won't have the same capabilities as you, and won't see any of your fancy changes.

## Web Surfing

- Make sure your computer has plenty of memory and a fast modem. Ensure your online service has high-speed internet connection capabilities. Your time is valuable and will slip away with slow, ineffective tools.

- When you visit a web page that you want to return to, bookmark it. If you're an America Online user, store this website in your "Favorite Places." If you're on another online service, save the website as your service provider allows. If this option isn't available to you, simply make a list of the web addresses and the titles of the web pages. Keep this list near your computer for quick reference.

- Sometimes, the time of day that you choose to surf the web has a lot to do with how productive your web surfing time will be. If the net is really busy, it will take you much longer to get from one web page to another. If you run into this problem, try surfing earlier or later in the day.

- Learn both basic and advanced search specifications when using search engines such as Excite, Alta Vista or Yahoo. You'll be able to find what you need quickly and without having to sift through hundreds of results.

- If there's a web page you always visit, make that your computer default page. For instance, if you always go directly to Yahoo, simply set your online software up so that you always go to that page every time you go online.

- Open up another window when you're downloading something. Rather than twiddling your thumbs waiting for it to finish, you can open up another window and work on something else at the same time.

- You may want to turn off your computer graphics, sound, and animation options, if all you're looking for is information. Web pages will load much quicker.

- If you have your own web page, save time by writing your html code offline and then uploading it later.

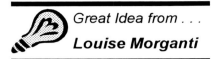

### Great Idea from . . . Louise Morganti

*I get a ton of e-mail at work, which I used to save in folders by topic—project, committee, etc. However, I found that if I didn't get an e-mail for a while on a topic, I'd make a new folder with a different name. After a while I had so many folders, I couldn't find anything.*

*I started to notice that when I wanted to find something, I thought about what else was happening at the time. So I reorganized all e-mail by month, including sent items. I keep a rolling year and clean out next month's about midway through each month (e.g. mid-April, I start looking at May mail).*

*If there is something I feel I still want to keep, I put it into one of two folders:*

1) ***Old Mail**: which I prune often*

2) ***Keepers**: there's not a lot in there, but while I could lose the "Old Mail" folder with just a small pang wondering what I've lost, I'd be upset about losing stuff in "Keepers"*

*I try to delete things right away that I know I don't need. I also move everything that's not an action item into the current month right away. I love having an in-box with only a dozen items!*

*I've been working with my boss to help him get his e-mail under control. We found that the monthly time frames don't work for him. When looking for something, he tends to think about who sent it to him, so we're trying to organize his e-mail by person.*

Louise Morganti
Quincy, MA

# E-mail Log

Make copies of this page and use it as your E-mail Log or duplicate a similar form on your computer.

Simply write in e-mail addresses that you regularly send e-mail to. Include any additional notes needed to jog your memory.

| Name | E-Mail Address | Notes |
|---|---|---|
| | | |
| | | |
| | | |
| | | |
| | | |
| | | |
| | | |
| | | |
| | | |
| | | |
| | | |
| | | |
| | | |
| | | |
| | | |
| | | |
| | | |

# Website Log

Make copies of this page and use it as your Web Site Log or duplicate a similar form on your computer.

When you visit a website that you want to save, simply write the relevant information on this log. Tip: If you're prompted to choose a user name and/or password when you visit a site, keep that information here for easy retrieval. Choose the same user name/password each time you can, unless specific circumstances will not allow it.

| Website Name | Website Address (URL) | UserName | Password |
|---|---|---|---|
| | | | |
| | | | |
| | | | |
| | | | |
| | | | |
| | | | |
| | | | |
| | | | |
| | | | |
| | | | |
| | | | |
| | | | |
| | | | |
| | | | |
| | | | |
| | | | |
| | | | |
| | | | |
| | | | |

# Chapter 58

# Goals and Personal Achievement

Achievement and success are based on internal monitors. Sure, someone may look at you and say that you're financially successful. Another may say that your job promotions prove you've achieved great feats in business. However, it all boils down to how you feel about yourself. Believe me, for every goal and achievement you reach, the more success you're going to feel inside. The more success you feel inside, the more you're inclined to reach even higher.

Setting goals is crucial. If you don't set goals for yourself, how will you ever know where you're going? People that have a clear destination in mind, short-term and long-term, always have a greater chance of reaching it. They may not reach it the first try, but with motivation and drive, they're certain to succeed at whatever they're trying to do.

- Make a list of the things you're currently spending your time on. Label each either A, B or C.

    ❖ A = Highly contributes to my goals and dreams
    ❖ B = Somewhat contributes to my goals and dreams
    ❖ C = Doesn't contribute to my goals and dreams at all

*Hint:* To achieve your goals and dreams, "eliminate" the C's! Remember that your time is precious and priceless. Spend it doing the things that get you closer to your ultimate goals!

• Take the time to learn how to do something, before just haphazardly jumping in. Think through your strategies. Ask questions. Read directions. Talk to experts. In doing so, you have an excellent chance of succeeding quicker.

• Accomplishment is a great motivator. Every single accomplishment provides the fuel for more.

• Don't major in minors. Spend your time on the things that get you closer to your dreams.

- Decluttering doesn't just refer to the physical excess stuff in homes and offices. It also refers to less tangible things that waste our time—bad relationships, paper shuffling, doing things that don't bring us closer to our goals.

- Stop focusing on extenuating circumstances. Focus on what you can control.

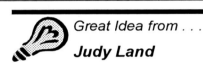

*Great Idea from . . .*

***Judy Land***

*When setting goals make sure they are well thought out and realistic.*

Judy Land
Sturgis, MI

- Don't cry over spilled milk. One of the most useless ways to use time is to spend it fretting over an outcome that can't be changed.

- Anything we haven't thought or done, something new, lies outside the parameters of our comfort zone—the personal area of thoughts and actions within which we feel comfortable and safe. When we consider doing new things, we often feel uncomfortable. And after feeling uncomfortable, we sometimes get discouraged and tend to give up before even starting something new. Of course, to accomplish something new, to reach our goals and to achieve our dreams, we're required to venture outside of our comfort zone. The achievement of your goals and dreams is completely up to you.

- Don't live your life without goals. Set your own personal goals for self-improvement, relationships, career, financial, health, family, education, social, spiritual and professional.

- Set goals that encourage growth, but are still attainable. Instead of saying you're going to save $100, you might set a mini-goal of $10 a week.

- Winston Churchill took daily naps, even during the height of World War II. If possible, incorporate a 15-minute nap into your daily routine. To play it safe, set your alarm clock. A power nap may be all you need to feel refreshed and ready to take on the world.

- Limit the amount of your television viewing each week. Moderate viewing is relaxing and enjoyable, but excessive viewing just eats up your precious time.

- If you only choose to spend your time doing those things that give you immediate gratification, you're going to miss out on many opportunities. The good things in life take time.

- Mood can greatly affect your productivity. When you find yourself in a bad mood, take a short break. Go for a walk. Go for a run. Call a friend. Do whatever it takes to cheer up, so that you are in the right state of mind to produce.

- Know where your time goes. It may be advantageous to keep a time log of everything you do for a minimum of two weeks. You might be surprised to see what's eating up your day and you'll be able to pinpoint what to eliminate. You're sure to find opportunities to increase your productivity.

- Get out of bed 30 minutes early to do something relaxing or motivational, such as stretching, savoring a good cup of coffee, reading the newspaper or listening to an uplifting radio or audio program.

- Don't recreate the wheel. Learn from someone who has knowledge, expertise and experience and follow his or her lead.

---

***Don't do something just because "that's the way it has always been done."***

Once upon a time, a child stood and watched her mother prepare the annual holiday ham. The mother carefully cut each end off the ham before placing it in the pan.

The child asked, "Mother, why do you always cut the ends off the ham?" The mother replied, "Well, that's the way my mother always did it."

So, the child called her grandmother and asked, "Grandma, why do you always cut the ends off the ham?"

The grandmother replied, "because that's the way my mother always did it."

Finally, the child called her great-grandmother and asked, "Great-Grandma, why did you always cut the ends off the ham?"

The great-grandmother replied, "Because the hams were too big to fit in my baking pan!"

Obviously, the mother and the grandmother were performing a system—cutting the ends off the ham—just because that's the way they thought it had to be done. Whereas, the only reason the great-grandmother was doing it, was because the ham couldn't fit in her pan!

So, what's the point of this little story?

Many people perform many tasks in their day. There's a very good chance, though, that they've never asked themselves why they're performing these tasks. Or if they're really necessary. Or if there may be a way to perform them better or in less time.

Continuously reevaluate your time and how you're using it, and chances are, you'll be sure to find areas that could be streamlined, improved or eliminated.

- Look for things you can combine to save time and accomplish more. For example, walk your dog and you'll also be exercising at the same time. Go to the beach with a motivational tape and you'll be relaxing and getting inspired simultaneously.

- Place a dollar value on your time. This will help you determine what you are willing, or not willing, to spend your time on. Don't ever sell yourself short. Establish how much your time is worth and use that value to make decisions on how to spend it.

- Find an object that represents the ultimate goal you are trying to accomplish. Leave it on your desk, or right where you'll see it at least once a day. It will help you to focus on that goal.

- Think about what you really want to be doing with your life. Your first step is to dream a little. What would make your life perfect? Make a wish list of everything you'd like in life that would make you happy.

- Translate your dreams into SMART goals:

  **S**pecific

  **M**easurable

  **A**ttainable

  **R**elevant

  **T**imely.

- Always make time for the things that matter most.

- Break up your goals into a series of mini-goals. Breaking your major goals down into smaller SMART goals will contribute to the accomplishment of those major goals. Don't forget to set deadlines for each one and reward yourself along the way.

- Focus on gain, rather than pain. Instead of being discouraged by the amount of work, focus on how it will feel when you've accomplished your goal or completed the project.

- The only way to save time, is to waste less time. The next time you hear yourself saying that you can't spare a minute, it's time to collect your thoughts and re-evaluate how you can work smarter so that you have plenty of time to reach your goals and dreams.

- Accentuate the positive. Eliminate the negative. Negative thoughts will bring you down and work against you. Positive thoughts give you energy and motivation.

- Don't get caught up in somebody else's schedule. Control your time, rather than being controlled by it and your accomplishments will follow.

- Some people work better and get a lot more done by playing classical music in the background. Try it.

- If you don't take the time to prioritize—make time for your ultimate goals—then all your time will be used up by less important things.

- The next time you say, "Someday I'll . . ." immediately schedule a date to *start doing it.*

- Strive for your goals. Do more of the things that are contributing to the achievement of your goals and less of what aren't.

- Have some fun. Schedule some pleasant things throughout your day, such as reading or walking. Even a few 15-minute breaks can work wonders. Doing so will improve your attitude and energy.

- Have fun by turning everything you do into a game. Set mini-goals and reward yourself for every one you reach. It will make you feel great about all you have accomplished.

- Stress can slow you down. Practice good humor. Laugh. Do something funny. Watch something funny. You only have one life. Enjoy it!

- Many people don't plan for the future. They are living in the *live for today* world. Unfortunately, lacking a vision for the future will limit your success. Determine what's important in the long-term, and you'll know what you should be working on in the short-term.

- Life is what you make of it. If you strive to live a happy life, you will be happy. Be thankful for the great gifts you have been blessed with—your life, your health, your family and friends, your happy memories. Don't focus on the things that bring you down. Rather, continuously strive to improve, and focus on the good things in life.

- Don't settle. Always do a little more than required. You'll be motivated and inspired to do more.

- Hiring an assistant to help you may be one of the best investments you'll ever make. There are people out there who can juggle a number of projects and tasks at once, without getting frustrated and without forgetting important details. A reliable, organized person can help you keep on track. He or she can be responsible for keeping your calendar up to date, scheduling appointments and arranging for events.

- Organize and clean-up your relationships. This includes a

**Great Idea from . . .**
**Jenette K. Rotatori-Zubero**

*If you don't happen to be among "the organized," here are three things that could help:*

*1) Take the opportunity to ease into it. Organize just one thing a day, or one a week. For example, one week organize your dresser drawers and the next week organize your office files.*

*2) Take the opportunity to get professional help. Did you know there are actually people willing to help you get organized? What a concept! Do yourself a favor and get someone to help.*

*3) Take the opportunity to purge. Just walk through your office and home. Throw out everything you don't use or donate it. That alone will free up a ton of space.*

*Organization can certainly help you free up time for both your professional and personal demands.*

Jenette K. Rotatori-Zubero
DreamWorks Coaching, Inc.
"The Power is YOU!"
http://www.dreamworkscoach.com

> *No dream is too high for those with their eyes in the sky.*
>
> Buzz Aldrin

marriage, friendship or any relationship that you have with other people. Make the most of your life by spending it with people you enjoy being around.

- If you're spending your life trying to change someone, there's a great chance that you're wasting an enormous amount of time and energy. It's a nearly impossible task. Most often people you are trying to change, don't want to change. If they really wanted to, they would have done so already.

- Don't waste time complaining. Problems are meant to be solved.

- Expand your interests. There is a great, big world out there, waiting to fill your heart and mind.

- Strive to always make people around you feel good. You'll feel great for doing so.

- Don't let others pile things on. Just because you *can* do it, doesn't necessarily mean you *should* do it. Learn to say "No." Admit it when you're too busy to take on something else.

- Be honest with your friends. If you must limit your time with them to a few hours on Thursday or Saturday, say so. If they're truly your friends, they'll understand. Respect their time limitations also.

- Slow down and enjoy. Don't let your life pass you by without taking in the beauties of nature. Relax and watch a sunset. Go to the beach in the evening and just listen to the waves roll in. Spend the day in the park with your family; have a relaxing picnic.

- Save one day a month for yourself. Use it to do whatever you want. Never let anything take priority over this day, except for a life and death emergency.

- Surround yourself with positive, happy, goal-oriented people; those that always make you smile and lift your spirits. Watch positive television programs. Listen to positive-thinking tapes.

- Motivate yourself. Read an inspirational quote first thing in the morning. Get inspired and your productivity is bound to skyrocket!

- As Winston Churchill once said, "Never, never, never give up."

- Ask questions. Learn at least one new thing each day. Share what you learned with someone else.

- Visit the Get Organized Now! website for your daily dose of inspiration. http://www.getorganizednow.com

- Always keep this book nearby to reference so you can stay organized! Effective organization clears the path to ultimate achievement. You'll be able to do whatever you set out to accomplish!

# Chapter 59

# Staying Organized

Y ou can't just organize once and then be done with it. Organization is an ongoing process; not an end result, one of continuous evaluation and improvement. Once you get organized, here are some ideas to help you stay organized.

- Designate one day a month, "Organizing Day." Put it on your calendar. When this day arrives, make a concerted effort to organize your office. Declutter your home. Slay the raging, paper beast. Thin out your file folders. Donate unwanted items. Organize. Organize. Organize. Then, organize some more!

- If you wait to organize until you have the time "to do the job right and in its entirety," you'll never get started. Organize yourself by listing tasks you can complete in shorter periods of time. Then schedule those tasks and do them.

- If you are having a hard time motivating yourself to organize, perhaps a friend, family member or associate would be willing to help. Maybe you could barter with them.

- Pay someone to help you organize. There are many professional organizers available if you choose. If you're on a tight budget, perhaps you could hire a student for a few hours to help.

- Take 10 minutes at the end of your day to tidy up. You'll be ready to start fresh the next day.

- Take advantage of the most effective organizing publications and tools. *Hint:* Visit my Get Organized Now! website. It's updated often and includes lots of great stuff to help you.

  http://www.getorganizednow.com

- Post a question or share your favorite ideas on the Get Organized Now! Discussion Forum. Simply visit the Get Organized Now! website and click on the FORUM link. Our reader community offers great questions and advice. Sharing helps us all achieve greater organizational success!

- Keep this book, *Finally Organized, Finally Free* nearby. It is meant to be read and referenced whenever you need a refresher on staying organized.

*Do, or do not.*
*There is no "try."*
Yoda

# Chapter 60

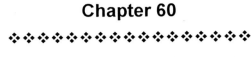

# The 10 Commandments of Finally Organized, Finally Free

## I wish you great success!

I hope you have enjoyed this journey we've taken together.

Please let me know how you're doing in your efforts to organize your life.

Drop me an e-mail with any questions or comments. I'd love to hear from you.

ebscompany@aol.com

I wish you the best of luck and success on your path towards being,

*Finally Organized, Finally Free!*

Maria Gracia, Author

I _____,
              (your name)
on this date _____,
                          (date)
do hereby solemnly swear to accept and abide by the following 10 Commandments so that I can be *Finally Organized, Finally Free.*

[1]    Thou shalt not give yourself the opportunity to generate clutter, physical or mental, for it will trap you into living a life of chaos.

[2]    Thou shalt always have a place for everything, and thou shalt put everything back where it belongs immediately.

[3]    Thou shalt always write it down, rather than committing details to memory alone.

[4]    Thou shalt clear out obstacles barring you from reaching your goals and achieving your dreams by simplifying.

[5]    Thou shalt not attempt to do everything yourself. Get help from family members, friends, associates and professionals.

[6]    Thou shalt spend a minimum of a few minutes each day organizing, tidying up, planning and scheduling.

[7]    Thou shalt not procrastinate. Do what you say you're going to do when you say you're going to do it. Control your destiny.

[8]    Thou shalt take care of yourself and your health. Make time for yourself and your loved ones. Laugh a little; love a lot. Enjoy life!

[9]    Thou shalt strive to have a positive outlook on life and an "I can do it" attitude.

[10]   Thou shalt keep this book handy for future reference. In addition, thou shalt visit the Get Organized Now! website often for new organizing ideas, tips, articles, slideshows and inspiration.

http://www.getorganizednow.com

# Thanks!

## Contributors

I would like to thank the following people for contributing organizing tips, ideas and questions for this book:

## Want to be part of our future publications?

## Share your favorite organizing ideas and tips

We welcome your tips and ideas for getting organized for future hard copy and electronic books, reports, newsletters and informational guides.

Send your ideas to:

Maria Gracia
5650 W Wahner Ave #214
PO Box 240398
Milwaukee, WI 53223-9015

Email Address:
ebscompany@aol.com

Website:
http://www.getorganizednow.com

# Index

# *Finally* Organized *Finally* Free

Disorganization can actually "trap" you into living a life filled with stress, frustration and chaos. It can rob you of the precious time you should be spending enjoying your life.

By overcoming disorganization you can be set "free" to live the kind of life you've always dreamed of.

*"Finally Organized, Finally Free"* by writer, speaker and personal advisor, Maria Gracia, gives you the simple solutions to help you declutter your life, simplify, and find more time to spend on the things you love.

There are no theories or difficult concepts here. Every idea, tip and technique is simple, proven effective and ready for you to use immediately.

## *With Finally Organized, Finally Free, you'll finally discover...*

✓ the four simple ways to slay the "Raging Paper Beast"
✓ how to get twice as much done in half the time
✓ hundreds of "clutter-controlling" tips
✓ the seven steps to easy filing
✓ how to reduce junk mail by 60% or more
✓ the power of the 3 P's to effectively manage your time
✓ the "sure-fire," "never-forget" reminder system
✓ how to find any item in your office or home . . . *in 30-seconds or less*
✓ the secret to get your children into the organizing "game"
✓ great ways to slash hours off of your housework time
✓ how to find time for that long-needed vacation
✓ with over 1,300 tips, you know there's much more!

## ABOUT THE AUTHOR

**Maria Gracia**, founder of Get Organized Now!, specializes in helping people get better organized to live the kind of stress-free life they've always dreamed of.

Originally from the east coast, Maria had an accomplished career as a marketing, organization and management specialist with Dun and Bradstreet's Nielsen Media Research in New York.

Today, Maria and her husband, Joe, live in Milwaukee, Wisconsin where they own and operate their company, Effective Business Systems. Maria founded the Get Organized Now! division in 1996.

Maria is an author, speaker, consultant and personal organizer. She is the author of the *Get Organized Now! Newsletter* and *Better Business*. Her broad range of skills covers planning, scheduling, peak productivity, records management, space planning, time and paper management, administrative services and computer oriented organizational systems.

http://www.getorganizednow.com

Cover Design by Joseph G. Gracia

**BlueMoon Publishing**
5650 West Wahner Avenue #214
PO Box 240398
Milwaukee, WI 53223-9015

ISBN 0-9672795-0-X